PAUL C. CLAYTON

Letters to Lee

MENTORING THE NEW MINISTER

AN ALBAN INSITUTE PUBLICATION

Library of Congress Card Number 99-72202
ISBN 1-56699-212-5

CONTENTS

97160

Values behind Leadership

May 19

Dear Lee,

These past two years while you have been a seminarian on our staff at First Church, you and I have become friends. You and Chris have often shared a meal with Jackie and me in our home. Today, as I saw you graduate, I was proud of you and confident that the church of the future will be well served by you and your classmates. After the commencement exercises, you said you were anxious about beginning your ministry at Central Church. You put it this way: "After graduation from seminary, after the congregation has called me, after ordination, after the moving van has come and gone, what do I do on that first Monday morning?"

I remember experiencing that same anxiety in 1959, when I began as pastor of a small congregation in rural Massachusetts. No other clergy told me how they organized their ministry. By trial and error, with the help of dozens of mentors and colleagues, I scratched out a discipline that worked for me.

The way we pastors work week by week, year after year, says more about what we believe than our term papers in Theology 101. I have come to hold certain values as tenets of faith. Here is my suggestion for the first Monday—in fact the first several Mondays—in your new church.

- Pull together a stack of information about the church—bylaws, annual reports, budgets, orders of worship, copies of the last few newsletters. You will probably find a history of the congregation written for an anniversary some years ago. Your predecessor and the interim minister may have left some notes or files. Bring all this material together and take time to read it. That pile of paper represents the first value: *Respect the congregation.* Laypeople are called by God to be the church as surely as we are called to be ordained ministers of the church. Martyred German theologian Dietrich Bonhoeffer, in his book *Life Together,* wrote:

> A pastor should not complain about his congregation, certainly never to other people, but also not to God. A congregation has not been entrusted to us in order that we should become its accuser. . . . [The] Christian community is like the Christian's sanctification. It is a gift of God which we cannot claim.[1]

- Gather together information about the community—a history of the town, reports from local government agencies, material from the chamber of commerce, a list of people and agencies to which you will refer people, a list of local clergy. This pile of paper represents the second value: *Ministry is a team effort.* When I play the Lone Ranger riding in to save the situation, I am usually building up my own ego, not the Body of Christ. Our ministry is authentic and lasting only if we establish a partnership with the community we serve.
- Pull together some of the books you will use every day: a Bible, a hymnal, the service book, some of the devotional books that have become good friends over the years. These books represent the third value: *mission.* Mission is not an alternative for those who might be interested. *Missio Dei,* "the mission of God," is what the faithful church is about. The church's temptation is to become a club. It is easier to live on the surface of life, to work on the horizontal plane. What is God doing in the world? That is the vocational quest of every Christian and every congregation. This stack of books is a reminder of the search for the mission to which God is calling us.
- Finally, return to your ordination service and reread the vows. They contain a rich mix of values that will have a different meaning for every season of your life. In our tradition we are ordained as "pastor and teacher." But we do not do these two separately: visit the hospital and teach the Bible study class. The two are inseparable.

The pastor is a teacher in the midst of chaos, and the teacher is a pastor in the confirmation class. Every conflict can become a teachable moment. We are called to embrace and make use of each of those moments as they are given. The ordination service also reminds us to build time into our daily lives for Bible study, reflection, and prayer. All of these elements represent the fourth value of your ministry: *the great traditions of the historic and ecumenical church.*

From these suggestions you can see that I think your question, "What do I do on Monday morning?" is an important one. Driving home from your ordination, I wondered how I could help you answer it.

Let me offer another suggestion. How would it be if, in this first year of your ministry, I corresponded with you about the issues you face at Central Church? I would share my practical, day-to-day habits of ministry with you in the hope that my experience would help you establish a pattern of ministry that is uniquely yours. We would both gain from this endeavor. You would see how I do it, and in writing to you, I would evaluate and sharpen the practice of ministry for myself.

I only ask you to remember that I would share these insights with you not because mine is the *only* right way to do ministry. It is the right way for *me* to do ministry, and I will often urge you to adopt my approach. It has worked for me, and I want you to see the benefit of doing it my way. But I know you are different from me and need to invent your own system. When you vehemently disagree or find that my suggestions simply don't work for you, don't feel guilty—invent a different way! For example, I suffered from a learning disability as a child. To accomplish a reading assignment, I had to begin long before the due date. Over the years, that necessity has translated into a pattern of organization that has worked for me. You may be one who works best under pressure, under the gun of the deadline. Create a discipline that fits your lifestyle.

What do you think?

Paul

CHAPTER 1

Creating a Work Environment

May 26

Dear Lee,

I am delighted that you are eager to engage in this dialogue. I hope it will be useful to you. The act of writing these letters to you will, I am sure, force me to think about the practice of ministry in a fresh way.

Your graduation-day question, "What do I do on Monday morning?" is simple yet complicated. You are right to suggest that problems arise from a lack of structure in the profession. Between us, I believe that many pastors claim to be busy but fritter away so much time that they don't put in even a 40-hour work week. I often ask at the end of a day, "What have I accomplished today?"

Let's begin by thinking about how we organize our lives. The trick is to build your own structure into the profession. True, interruptions are often more important than your planned routine for the morning, but that doesn't mean you should have no plan. Having your work week organized doesn't mean you can't be flexible; it means you do not allow anyone and everyone to plan your time. How do we establish a sense of place, time, and community?

Place and time are the easy parts of the puzzle. We need a place where we can go to work on Monday morning. For me, the dining-room table of the parsonage doesn't do it. The refrigerator, novel, couch, and household chores are too visible there. I have always had an office in a church building where I have all I need to assist in my work—a library, a secretary, and a setting for conversation. But many church buildings are not heated on weekdays or are otherwise unconducive to work. In such cases, the congregation assumes that a room in the pastor's home will be used for work. If that becomes necessary, that workplace must be one where family life is not interrupted by work life, and vice versa. If there can be a separate entrance to the pastor's study, that is all the better.

How does one organize the week? Here is the pattern that works for me. In the morning I read at home for a few hours. I then go to the church office at about 9 or 9:30 and stay there until shortly after noon. After a full-hour lunch break, I visit in the parish most afternoons. Almost every evening (four to five nights a week) I am at a meeting or in a counseling session. Here is the general pattern of my morning schedule: Monday morning is administrative. Tuesday I try to get the sermon outline in place. I write the sermon on Wednesday morning and often into the afternoon; sometimes it takes all day Thursday as well. Friday morning is devoted to weekend preparation. Saturday is my day off. Sunday morning is filled with worship, teaching, and pastoral care, both during and after the coffee hour. Some Sunday afternoons and evenings are free; most are not. Sunday is a great time to visit hospitals in the city that are hard to reach in weekday traffic. It's also a good time to visit families. Pastors in smaller churches often have youth groups and confirmation classes to add to Sunday schedules.

Now, Lee, don't be discouraged by that schedule. The truth is that seldom does a week fit the plan precisely. Pastoral concerns break the pattern. Funerals, weddings, and help with personal crises interrupt the routine. You will find some of your most important ministry in those interruptions. Your personal agenda also can, and ought to, interrupt this schedule. The burden of evening meetings wears one down. I have never found a way to cut down on them. But I compensate by taking time to watch our children's after-school soccer game; I am no stranger to Fenway Park and the Boston Red Sox; Jackie and I find time now and then for a leisurely lunch at a nice restaurant. The point is, you need a plan, and the congregation needs to know its general outline so that people can feel free to talk to you at a time convenient for you.

The desk calendar is next to the Bible on my desk (more modern pastors have both Bible and calendar on their computers!). Imagine yourself sitting in the stewardship committee meeting in late spring. Out of that meeting comes a schedule, which you can create by planning back and forward from a specific event. Stewardship Sunday is the day pledges are gathered. Working back, write in the events that need to happen before that Sunday. Working forward, enter the follow-up events needed to bring the effort to a conclusion. The committee plan might look like this (begin reading at "November 8"; read up and then down):

September 8	Finance committee completes budget request
October 19 and 26	Training sessions for visitors
October 26-31	Leadership pledges made
October 28	Dinner invitation budget information mailed
October 30	Newsletter information
November 1	Dinner reservation deadline
November 7	Information dinner
November 8	*Stewardship Sunday*
November 9-15	Follow-up phone calls
November 15-22	Visitors call on homes of those not pledged
November 24	Pledge results submitted to finance committee
November 29	Celebrate success in worship

Now enter those dates in your personal calendar and the church calendar, along with dates generated by all other committees, boards, and organizations. Software programs can chart the sequence of events and automatically enter them on your computerized calendar. The wonderful thing about the computer is that other people can enter events in your calendar. You may groan at the thought of others scheduling your life for you, but if you block out times you need to reserve for yourself or for contingencies, the electronic calendar makes you more available in the church community. More important than your personal calendar is the office calendar. I will always remember the summer when two weddings were scheduled for the same hour on the same day in the same place. It was a nightmare! The office calendar is the instrument that prevents such schedule conflicts. Everyone needs to be trained to honor that calendar—clergy and laity alike.

Many feel that administration is a necessary evil to be gotten out of the way to make room for people. I believe that administration is the way a pastor includes laypeople in church leadership. "Lone Rangers" are apt to exclude people from the work of planning. If you're going to share the ministry, if you're going to build up the Body of Christ so that laypeople don't need to depend on you for everything, organize your life and the life of the institution to include them in the planning. Administration is a religious word: It derives from the word *ministry,* and we are called to "administer the sacraments." Administration is the way we include the whole people of God in sacrament and ministry.

This first pastorate is the most important of all, Lee. Here you will establish patterns of life that will become the assumptions for the rest of your ministry. I am not asking you to adopt my discipline of ministry. I am urging you to be intentional about your work habits. Decide how you will manage your days and weeks. The choices you make this first year will be with you for a long time.

Your fellow disciple in the discipline of ministry,

Paul

CHAPTER 2

Ministry with Others

June 2

Dear Lee,

Reading today's letter from you, I sensed that you are overwhelmed by all the decisions that must be made in these first weeks of your ministry at Central Church. I am sending this note by e-mail, for I want you to see right off that you are not alone. That is the saving grace in pastoral ministry—not only that the Holy Spirit is with us but that our colleagues in ministry are with us also.

The most obvious colleagues are those called to share the ministry with us on the church staff. How can you best lead the staff? Obviously, in a multiple-staff church, that is a large part of the senior minister's task, requiring weekly meetings and periodic retreats. But every pastor works with a staff. The smallest church has a sexton, an organist, a kid who mows the lawn, a treasurer who pays the bills, and a secretary.

Lee, I'm not sure Central Church has a secretary, but I am sure you need one. See if you can talk your board into hiring someone for at least a day or two a week to produce the order of worship and the newsletter. Even a volunteer is helpful. Not only do secretaries do the clerical work, they also hear what's going on in a congregation. People tell the church secretary what they would never say to the pastor.

I believe three things are true of church staffs:

- The senior minister's job is to lead the staff to become an open and dynamic team.

- Such a staff is able to lead the congregation into an equally open and dynamic life together.
- Even very small churches are led by a staff.

Consider your congregation, Lee. You are the sole pastor. You have a staff, and leading it is not an easy task. Communication can be difficult, even among clergy; it's much more complicated when the staff includes a young pastor, an elderly janitor, a secretary who is a young mother, and a musician who is trained to work alone and aspire to perfection. Together you lead the congregation. These staff meetings are vital, therefore, to the whole church. You remember from your days as a seminarian in this congregation that we met once a week for two or more hours.

Scheduling that meeting is hard in a small church; it needs to fit the schedules of those who work for the church part-time. Your staff will probably meet once a month, given those restrictions. Build an agenda that makes sense to all. Begin each meeting with creative worship, not an off-the-cuff prayer. It might be a reading, some Bible study, and a meditation. Nurture staff members until they are ready to take a turn at leading the others in worship. The meeting needs to be a time when members can share their plans, their gripes, and their worries. Going over the church calendar for the month ahead is a way to make sure that all know what is expected of them. This is also the setting where you can test some of your ideas and air your complaints and concerns.

I want to emphasize the importance of respect among a staff. If the secretary can't count on people getting material in by the deadline, if the sexton finds that a room cleaned yesterday was messed up that evening by a group he didn't know was to be in the building, if the organist doesn't know the worship theme for Sunday until after the Thursday choir rehearsal, if the treasurer gets bills a month late because the committee chair forgets to turn them in, if the pastor can't count on all these people to do their jobs—if that's the situation, the congregation as a whole will suffer. Frankly, I have found clergy to be the most disrespectful members of the church staff. That observation sounds harsh, but it is true. We clergy have a way of assuming that the deadline doesn't apply to us. I have often been surprised to see clergy order secretaries around, talk down to maintenance staff, and fail to consider the choir director's rehearsal schedule. If we break all the rules we set up to keep the staff working together, we can't expect anyone else to observe them.

I have often heard you speak of your friend John, an associate pastor in a large church. In one sense, his life is dramatically different from yours. Working in multiple-staff churches is hard for clergy. I brought together a dozen former seminarians to ask what they wished we had taught them before graduation. The startling revelation was that every person who became an associate or assistant minister after seminary was miserable. We clergy have been trained to be the center of attention.

Small and large congregations are radically different institutions. But when I, who served a large congregation, sat down with a skillful pastor of a small congregation to plan a course for seminary students on the practice of ministry, I was amazed to find that she and I organized our lives in almost exactly the same way. One of my former associates, Christina Braudaway-Bauman, has made a list of topics that she calls "A Survival Kit for Associate Ministers." In studying it, I recognized that it was also a survival kit for the senior minister. I bring it up because it also points to the way that your ministry in a small church and John's ministry in a multiple-staff church are similar. Here is Christina's list of topics with my comments on how each topic relates to both large and small churches.

1. A Collaborative Spirit

"Lone Rangers don't belong in ministry, especially on multiple staffs," Christina says. I have friends I respect whom Christina would probably call "Lone Rangers." They succeed in large churches by arranging the staff in a hierarchical way. Specialists in education, pastoral care, mission, and administration are called to be full- or part-time staff members responsible to the senior minister. They need respect. If they are to do well in their area of responsibility, that area needs to be clearly delegated to them. This arrangement works for many because everyone on staff is accountable to the senior minister. I work better with a staff that works *with* me rather than *for* me. I like a colleague who assumes sufficient parity to critique my work and keep me alive and growing.

In either a hierarchical or a collaborative staff, each person must respect the other. The senior minister who feels obliged to read the associate's sermon before it is preached shows a lack of respect. The associate who complains to friends about the bad theology of the senior minister but never confronts him or her directly likewise indicates a lack of respect. Lee, many pastors in your position don't respect lay leaders in the congregation, and thus are not respected by the members. When respect is absent, when we do not regard one another as colleagues, it is time for a long talk with a counselor, or it is time to upgrade your résumé.

2. A Job Description

Areas of primary responsibility should be defined. Both clergy and laity need to know who is responsible for what. If those expectations are put in writing, it is all the better.

3. Good Conflict-Management Skills

Christina says, "Refuse to participate in triangulation with members of the congregation, especially with those who may try to leave with you their complaints about your senior colleague, rather than dealing with him or her directly." We need to talk about conflict management in another letter. But here let me say that I have learned from hard experience. I once believed that conflicts should be resolved within the staff. In a particular staff of three, one seemed always to be the "odd one out." Finally, he found another church, where he would be the sole pastor. On the eve of his departure, he shared his bitterness about the experience over a few beers with the chair of the deacons, who told the whole board. The next day, when I heard from a dozen people what my colleague had said, I was furious and he was embarrassed. I learned from that experience that a staff cannot possibly resolve all conflicts by itself. Married people often need outside help; why not staff people? I learned also that the board of deacons' knowledge of the difficulty was not a catastrophe. In fact, many had already figured out what was going on, simply by watching us. From that moment on, we had an agreement that if any one of us on the staff thought it was needed, we would invite the denominational executive or the congregation's staff-relations committee to come and help us. Lee, when there is a conflict between you and your staff or the leading members of the congregation, that doesn't mean you should move on to another parish; it means someone needs to step in and help.

4. A Healthy Sense of Personal Authority

From her experience as an associate minister of two congregations, Christina says, "I believe that associate ministers have to earn the authority which congregations often simply grant to senior ministers. This is also a gender issue. I am convinced that women have to work harder to gain trust." While that may be true of associates and women, I believe that authority is always earned, not given. These first months at Central Church are a honeymoon period–time for the congregation to discover how talented you are, and time for you to discover how wonderful the congregation is. Christina's words speak to you as well as to your friend John in your different situations: "After you attend compassionately to a few families in crisis, preach a few good sermons, [and] plan a few well-run programs, your pastoral relationship, your authority, your ministry will grow."

5. A Support System

You may often feel it is a waste of time to attend the clergy association meeting or the fellowship group within the denomination. But you need a terrific group of colleagues with whom you can find support, trust, and honesty. It is not easy to find a group like that. Many clergy are too competitive to be helpful. Most of us have three or four groups of colleagues at the same time. Don't feel guilty about time spent with friends in the ministry. Every congregation knows you will be able to serve them best only if competent colleagues surround you.

6. Fair Compensation

The salary differential between senior and associate minister is telling. Within three years, we tried to bring the associate minister's salary up to 65 to 70 percent of the senior minister's salary. That was the denominational guideline where we lived. That differential was accomplished even though I had been with the congregation for 20 years and the associate had been there for 3 years. That decision seems unfair to some. But I believe it is the only way collegiality can be accomplished. Equity is also relevant in a small church. The remuneration of minister, secretary, janitor, musician, and treasurer needs to reflect some rational order if the relationships are to be whole.

Bob was a senior minister in the next town. I didn't know him well enough to call him a mentor, but I admired him and watched him carefully so that I could learn from his experience. His associate was a talented and popular figure. One day a small group of us, including Bob, were standing at the back of the room while Bob's associate captivated the audience. One of Bob's friends whispered to him, "How can you stand working with him? With his sex appeal and gift of gab, you look almost frumpy." Bob answered, "The more popular he is, the better I look. Every success he enjoys is a credit to me." I've never forgotten that exchange. It is true: We are not competitors; we are partners.

Partnership is a key word in ministry. Are we called to be partners with Christ? It is just as certain that we are called to be partners with our colleagues on the church staff and with the laity we serve.

Your colleague in ministry,

Paul

CHAPTER 3

Our Public and Private Lives

June 10

Dear Lee,

Thanks for your letter that came today. I'm glad you found my letter of
May 26 helpful. I understand your concern about fitting Fenway Park
into a pastor's schedule. How do we draw the line between work and
play, between our public and private lives? Let me tell you something
that happened the first year of my ministry: One spring day I was washing the windows of the garage. I heard my neighbor calling from her
kitchen door to her husband, "Bill, what's Paul doing?" Bill replied,
"He's washing the windows in his garage." Her response: "What's he
doing that for? We never look through those windows."

The pastoral ministry is a public life. I hear you describe Chris's
anxiety about how to deal with the congregation's expectations of the
pastoral spouse. Even in a time when many female pastors are married,
the old stereotype of "the minister's wife" haunts us. Will the two of
you have any privacy at all? If you become parents, how difficult will it
be for your child to be the preacher's kid? We've all heard stories about
the woes of the "PK"!

The pastor's life is a public life. I think we should be grateful for
that. Our witness is public. Every Christian is called to make a witness.
Our children, neighbors, and colleagues witness what we believe and
value. That witness makes a difference in the world. The pastor's public
life ensures that a whole community witnesses our life example. In ad-
dition, public life is an opportunity to make a difference in the lives of
people and the community. But public life is also a burden and can

become demonic, poisoning family life and turning the witness into a show of hostility so that what people learn from us is how *not* to live.

The good news is that we can control how public we want to be. In fact, you need to make decisions about certain issues in these first weeks of your ministry. Sit down with the official board of the church and talk about where you and Chris plan to draw the line between your public and private lives. Encourage your board to speak honestly about any problems the congregation will have with your plan. It may take a while to come up with mutually agreeable principles (in fact, it may require a compromise). Then go public with the plan in the church newsletter. Encourage people to talk about it, and insist that the official board defend the agreement along with you. If you don't initiate such a process, if you simply wait to see how things work out, then you will have decided not to decide where to draw the line between your public and private lives.

Let me give you some examples of what I mean by this "line":

- Chris is concerned about life in the parsonage. Jackie and I have found that living in a church-owned home is not desirable for us. When the hot-water heater needs to be replaced, the disclosure can become an opportunity for members to ask if we take too many showers. Actually, I don't think it matters who owns the house. If we are the owners, we risk hearing complaints that the residence is too posh for a minister or that the housing allowance is too generous. Either way, the pastor's home is going to be dragged into church politics. Nothing will immunize you from that outcome, except a clear agreement that neither you nor Chris will be a party to it.

- Talk with the official board about the financial problem the parsonage arrangement creates for you. While it is cheaper for the church to own the parsonage tax-free, that arrangement creates no opportunity for you to build equity that will allow you to move to a church that has no parsonage, or to retire to a home of your own. Jackie and I bought the cottage on Cape Cod, which is now a wonderful place to retire. I persuaded the last congregation I served to put aside seven percent of my salary and to invest it in an equity fund. Be sure to consult a tax attorney so that you will be able to roll the amount over into either a down payment or an IRA when you leave that church.

- You can't control what people say about you. If you have a public life, people will gossip about you. As a high school student our daughter went to France in an exchange program, and a female student from France came to visit us for three weeks. One day I came home for lunch to find this young woman upstairs in her bedroom with a male student, also from France. Nothing scandalous was happening, but I was angry with the school for not engaging these students in a program for the whole day. I conveyed my outrage to the director of the exchange program, and he agreed that some changes had to occur. The program did improve, and the French students went home amid good feelings on everyone's part. Two weeks later, the chair of the board of deacons came to me to ask, "Paul, is it true that you and Jackie are getting a divorce?" I said that was not true, at least so far as I knew, and inquired why he was asking. He said a rumor going around the school suggested that I had come home for lunch and found Jackie in bed with a man. Lee, there is no way we can manage the gossip mill. I told the deacon about the exchange-student incident and assured him that time would prove the rumor groundless.

You may feel awkward talking with the board about your vacation and day off in the first month of your ministry, but you need to do just that. First of all, you and Chris need at least one full day together, away from church business. I have never worked seven days in a row. It's against our religion to do so. In a world where executives are expected to work 85 hours a week, we need to observe a Sabbath. Taking a day off from work is an important witness. Creativity diminishes when we work more than 50 hours a week. Monday, the typical clergy day off, has never worked for me. There are all those details that came up on Sunday that need immediate attention. Jackie works on Monday, and the children are in school. So I take Saturday off, since that is when the family is free. I always have the sermon done by Thursday and the liturgy in place by the end of the day on Friday. If there is a wedding on Saturday, I take the preceding Wednesday off. However you arrange your life, the congregation needs to know so that they can help you protect that precious time you have together.

The same is true of vacations. You followed my example and negotiated a five-week vacation so that you could take one week in the winter and four in the summer. But now you need to talk with the board about how they will implement that agreement. They need to provide in the budget not only for Sunday supply but also for pastoral care during the time you are away. I have always gone out of town for vacation. We camped all over the country and didn't mind imposing on family who lived in attractive places. If you spend your vacation in town, it's impossible to be unavailable when genuine need arises in the parish. Really get away from it all.

If you tell people how you plan to organize your life to have some time to yourselves, the congregation will honor your private time. Be clear about when and where you will be available to them, how you feel about phone calls to the parsonage, when you will be visiting with hospital patients and with families. The more open you can be with the church about your work habits, the more people will help protect your leisure time.

The two of you will need to discover for yourselves other issues of relationships in that public-life/private-life tension apart from the official church board.

• Friendship with parishioners is a complicated issue. On the one hand, I don't believe a pastor should always be professional, official, and clad in a clerical collar. Jesus was a friend; why is that role impossible for us? On the other hand, being close to the pastor has an impact on the social dynamic of laypeople, and we fool ourselves if we think a pastor can be totally open with friends in the parish. When a group of us talked over lunch before a clergy-association meeting, it became clear that the subject is controversial. Some were convinced that friendships get in the way of faithful ministry. Others were equally sure that clergy need to get out of their ivory towers and make friends with people—"the way Jesus did," the rabbi said with a grin. This is not a simple issue, Lee. You and Chris need to make some decisions. For me it comes down to the health of the pastor and the pastor's family. When I was a second lieutenant in the Army, I felt that the officers club was ingrown. In time I came up with a theory. These military people moved every three years, often to posts overseas. It was painful to say good-bye to friends made off base, so they made the Army their life. It isn't that such a choice is evil; living in a narrow subculture is simply boring. The most interesting people I knew in the Army and in the ministry had a life off base.

- One of our ordination vows is that confidences will be kept. I don't share confidential information with Jackie. If she really doesn't know a confidential piece of information, she won't have to pretend she doesn't know. Yet, in some circumstances, she has to know. For example, if I think someone has a crush on me, I consult Jackie because she is able to help me differentiate between my ego and reality. We are all vulnerable here, Lee. Anyone can accuse us of sexually abusing him or her, and we are in trouble. A close relationship with our lifelong partner is the only safety there is.

- One of my former students went to the dump early on a Saturday morning, dressed in her worst jeans and sweatshirt, with her hair standing on end. Right next to her she saw the chair of the board of deacons dressed in a sleek warm-up suit. Should she have felt embarrassed? For me, learning about the dress code is not the point. The point is that we live a public life, even at the dump. Life will be a whole lot easier if we can grow to the point of being comfortable with our private lives in public. We might have to change some of the habits we developed in high school, and our parishioners might have to change some of their assumptions about clergy. In my opinion, it doesn't mean we have to dress up for the dump run.

- Jackie and I remember Laura, the 20-year-old victim of an abusive family whom I tried to help. After some weeks of counseling, I invited her home for supper one evening. She became a baby-sitter, shared meals with us often, and was virtually a member of our extended family. Laura was not able to manage the arrangement. She imagined she was my lover and became hostile toward Jackie. I had to sever the social relationship, and she left our family and the church with a deep sense of rejection. Including Laura in our family was inappropriate. It hindered her healing.

You can see the difficulties. One question I find helpful is "Whose problem is this?" If a parishioner has trouble seeing me with a glass of wine in hand on Jackie's and my wedding anniversary, I think that is the parishioner's problem, not mine. But if I can't see any separation between my private life and the public ministry, I have a huge problem.

If we are not clear about this distinction, we end up with burnout on the one hand or abuse on the other. Pastoral theologian William H. Willimon asserts that it is meaninglessness that produces burnout.[1] Most of us assume that overwork, stress, and never being able to take a day off are what sour our sense of vocation. I think Willimon is right in saying it is none of those things but rather the overwhelming sense that what we do makes no difference. I would suggest also that burnout grows out of professionalism. When the ministry is no longer a calling, when it is a job with no connection to our faith, when we don't put ourselves into our work, when being a pastor has nothing to do with who we are as a person —then there is no reason to continue. Any one of a dozen other professions is more rewarding. On the one hand, therefore, burnout occurs when the ministry doesn't matter to us anymore.

On the other hand, abuse occurs when the public ministry is totally personalized. A parishioner falls in love with us. *Transference* is the psychological term for it. That infatuation has nothing to do with us. It is "the pastor" who is the object of the affection. If we maintain no clear distinction within ourselves between the public and the private life, we fall into abuse. If we enter an intimate and sexual relationship with a counselee or parishioner, we are guilty of abuse. A sexual relationship between boss and secretary, senator and lobbyist, counselor and patient, pastor and parishioner, is abuse. You and I both know instances of a pastor who fell in love with a parishioner, married that person, and remained happily married for many decades. But in these last years, as we have become aware of abuse in our society and in the church, things have changed.

I was single during the first three years of my first pastorate. Even then, my rule was that I would not date anyone in the congregation. Many parents hoped that something would happen between their daughter and me. This "no dating parishioners" rule of mine was helpful. I often wondered what I would do if I fell in love with a woman in the congregation. Would I hold fast? I remember thinking that if I could not, I would cut short my ministry in that church. That was in 1959. An intimate sexual relationship is all the more unacceptable in the ministry today. If a pastor falls in love with a parishioner, he or she needs to resign as pastor, and both individuals need to leave that church. Even then, the congregation will be left bruised and divided. How can I emphasize this point more strongly? Be clear about the boundary between your private life and your public ministry.

You can see the importance of this line between public and private life, Lee. It is good that you have brought it up early in your ministry. This issue will haunt all of us until the end. One final story from my experience illustrates the point.

I was only 32 years old when I moved to serve a large, multiple-staff congregation. A woman with a strong personality was in charge of the youth ministry. I tried in every way to share that ministry with her, with no success. It was her domain, and there was no room for me. "These are my kids, not yours," she said. As I watched her encourage the young people to become dependent on her, I began to feel that this turf war was sick. I talked with the committee responsible for the youth ministry. The committee joined me in talking with her, asking other advisors to join her, and in every way possible tried to overcome this barrier between her and me. Nothing worked. At the end of the year, the committee members and I were unanimous. We told her she would not be advisor in the fall. She declared war on me. "If I go, I will make sure you go, too."

That was the worst summer of my life. Jackie and I were expecting our second child in September. I was sure that this woman could deliver on her promise to end my ministry in that church. I was papering and painting the nursery in the parsonage one August afternoon. The man who had volunteered to join this woman in advising the youth was sitting on a stool listening to me vent my fury and worry. I heard myself say to him: "My life is the ministry. If she ends my ministry, she ends my life." I saw the folly of my words the moment they were spoken. If I left the ministry, I would still be husband and father. I would still be me. I could make a living some way. In that moment I understood the difference between my public and my private life, the distinction between my job and my identity, the separation of my work and myself. In that moment I was free—free to risk my ministry for what I felt was right.

You probably know what happened. The committee and I stuck to our guns. She left her position as youth advisor. Her war against me fizzled; she never had any power over me, except in my own mind. I tell this story with deep sadness. She left the church that fall, and died suddenly the next spring. I wonder how the story would have ended if I had known in the beginning what I learned in the end. Had I recognized the boundary between my ministry and my life at the beginning, would she have behaved differently? I think both of us had the same problem. We both believed that our lives depended on our ministry in that church.

If I had been free of that idolatry, I might have been able to liberate her.
But we'll never know.

Yours in the friendship we share in Christ,

Paul

CHAPTER 4

Leadership Style

June 18

Dear Lee,

Don't apologize for writing so soon and often. You have a steep learning curve ahead of you. You have so much to think through this summer. I would bet you'll be so absorbed in the work by September that you will forget my address. I think your idea of holding a church board meeting in the week before Labor Day is a good one. It gives you a little time to get your mind straight.

But you wrote with a young parishioner, Donna, in mind. I understand the situation to be this: Donna was arrested for shoplifting at the drugstore. Her arrest caused many people to wonder if she is also the one who has stolen purses from the choir room during worship and money from the petty-cash drawer in the office. The group that came to report this matter to you was most worried about Donna's father, the moderator of the congregation. He is, I gather, a controlling, opinionated man, and the group feared that his frustration with Donna would hurt the church. "He'll take out his anger with Donna on us," they said. That's why they want you to deal with the situation. This incident raises the issue of leadership style and is, therefore, a great follow-up to my last letter.

This situation brings to mind a wonderful book I read some time ago, *The Equipping Pastor,* by R. Paul Stevens and Phil Collins,[1] which takes a family-systems approach to congregational leadership. I recommend it to you. All things considered, Donna would seem to represent a classic case for family therapy. The systems approach would understand

Donna to be the designated victim in this situation. She is probably as afraid of her father as the whole congregation is. The systems approach would treat the dynamic of the family so that Donna, her father, and other family members might get at the cause of the hurtful behavior. Families get caught in triangular relationships. Could it be that instead of dealing directly with Donna, her father expects her mother to intercede? This triangle can never work, since it creates a victim (Donna) who feels persecuted by the villain (the father) and positions the mother to assume the role of rescuer. Everyone in the triangle loses. In treating the family, in restoring healthy and direct relationships, the family-systems approach is able to help everyone.

It seems to me that the church is also a dysfunctional family in this incident. In the opinion of this delegation, Donna is the victim, her father is the villain, and you are to come to the rescue so that church members won't have trouble with the moderator. It sounds like a classic triangle to me, and you are being set up as rescuer. What should be your proper leadership role in this situation? How can the church family, as a system, help Donna and her family?

A great many images of pastoral leadership are taught in seminaries these days. Here are a few:

- We should be the *chief executive officer*, the boss. Many churches would gladly have you adopt that role, but the downside is steep indeed. The CEO is easily fired when things go bad, and if you play that role, no one else will feel obliged to stand beside you as a partner in the ministry of Jesus Christ.

- We should be the *teacher*. The role of rabbi or professor offers an attractive leadership style. It allows one to be the authority of the faith and to let others lead the institution. But that dualism is inconsistent with the Incarnation. In fact, I have never known a responsible professor or rabbi who doesn't share in the leadership of the institution.

- We should be the *coach*. The idea of calling the plays from the sidelines is the perfect picture of safety. But can you imagine leading a church without ever getting mud on your uniform, without ever being on the line beside a parishioner?

You can go on with the images. The family-systems approach to leadership is worth considering, Lee. Listen to the leadership theory of Stevens and Collins:

> The most direct way to equip the saints for the work of ministry is not to devise strategies for equipping individuals but to equip the church (as a system). Then the church will equip the saints.[2]

> God did not give pastor-teachers "to do the work of ministry" as implied in the KJV. . . . The so-called "fatal comma" in some English translations led to a clerical understanding that pastor-teachers were given by God, first, for the equipment of the saints, and second, to do the work of ministry. But the comma is supported neither by the text nor the context. Rather, pastor-teachers were given to the church *to equip the saints to do the ministry.*[3]

> A man in a museum looking at the colossal skeleton of a dinosaur that once roamed the earth triumphantly turned to the woman beside him and asked, "What happened? Why did they die out?" She answered, "The climate changed."[4]

In the short run, I suppose you did something—went to the police station, went to the father's office, asked the church delegation to go with you. You managed just fine. But leadership, as differentiated from management, is the art of changing the climate, the culture, the system, so that there will be no more need to designate victims or rescuers.

You can see the outline of your task this summer in the work of Stevens and Collins. The leader must be within the system. The first thing you must do is join the Christian community called Central Church. Only if you are yourself a member of that community will the members permit you to lead. Joining is more than an act, more than a liturgy—it is a matter of the heart. It's not easy. Some have never left their old church and, therefore, can't really join the new congregation. It is risky to join a church. Everyone assumes that the pastor will change the church, but if you really belong to that church, it will also change you. As Stevens and Collins point out, "Christian ministry is essentially covenant. There is a 'for better, for worse' about it, a bonding and binding agreement to work this thing out."[5] This whole summer—the sermons, the meeting with the board, and yes, even the situation with Donna—is all a honeymoon, a time for you to join that church and a time for the church to join you. This summer you need to think about what kind of leader you want to be.

The traditional question of leadership is framed in the following graph:

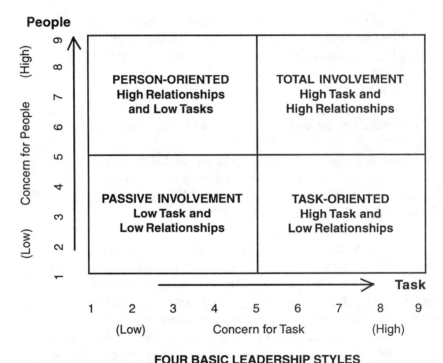

FOUR BASIC LEADERSHIP STYLES
(Stevens and Collins, *The Equipping Congregation,* 64)

When I first saw this graph 20 years ago, it was a measure of each person's preferred leadership style, with the understanding that each has a back-up style that kicks in when one is in a crisis. The systems approach to leadership understands that one's style can be adjusted to the context. We do this all the time: sometimes we are as task-oriented as a CEO; then we are as people-oriented as a pastoral counselor; later we are passive so that others can find their way; still again we are totally involved to jump-start the congregation. It's like paddling a canoe—now we paddle like mad in a sweeping "C" stroke, then we sit quietly using the paddle as a rudder, and in the sweetest moment of all, we lay the paddle down and just drift down the river enjoying the view.

I believe a crisis like Donna's arrest is a gift. It provides an opportunity to see the congregational system and to intervene appropriately. Your first impulse will be to try to minimize the conflict, to make sure Donna's father doesn't make trouble in the congregation. I'm sure you would like to fix the problem and thereby receive the approval of a grateful congregation. It's hard to step back and address the system instead of the symptom. A trusted colleague, a spiritual director, a supervisor, or a counselor often gives us the perspective we need in these situations. The truth is that this is a teachable moment. Again, to quote Stevens and Collins:

> The Chinese word for crisis is composed of two characters, one meaning "danger" and the other "opportunity." The systemic pastor welcomes the opportunity of every crisis. Sometimes he or she will provoke one.[6]

This issue of leadership style came clear to me in a seminar required for doctor of ministry candidates. It was my turn to offer a case study that would reveal my leadership style. The case pictured me, as pastor, making a presentation to the board of deacons on the way the doxology should be treated in worship. The case was not fiction.

Some in the congregation wanted to keep the last line of the doxology as it had always been sung: "Father, Son, and Holy Ghost." Others, who wanted more gender equity in our worship, felt that the last line should be sung as "Creator, Christ, and Holy Ghost." They argued that this alternative would allow both sides to sing different words together. The issue had been discussed for some months. It was time for the deacons to decide.

I summarized the argument for each alternative and added a third: that we substitute an entirely different doxology. The denominational book of worship had several possibilities. I told the deacons that I favored the third alternative: different words to different music—a different hymn. I then assured the deacons that it was their decision, and, of course, I would lead the congregation in whatever way they saw fit.

After a lengthy discussion, the board voted the second alternative: different words to the familiar tune. I ended the case study with the words: "I left the meeting content."

The D.Min. seminar discussed the case, some favoring one doxology, others favoring another. As the hour of adjournment was at hand, the professor said, with feeling, "Paul, you have abdicated the responsibility to lead. If there is no clear, winning word from the pastor, the congregation is doomed." The issue of leadership style had been defined in that classroom. The professor held to a hierarchical leadership style that would have the pastor lead; I advocated a family-systems style that insisted that the board of deacons take the lead. The alternative leadership styles were clear. I left the seminar content.

Your colleague in the ministry,

Paul

CHAPTER 5

Power in Ministry

June 23

Dear Lee,

I was delighted to get your e-mail message in response to my last letter
on leadership. I gather that the member of your church who is a retired
pastor didn't care for the family-systems style. I'm not surprised. To
someone trained in a different model of ministry, it might well seem that
I was urging you to surrender leadership, pass the buck to the laity, and
escape the risks and burdens of pastoral leadership to which we have
been called. For you to have two opposing ideas of ministry is a gift,
Lee. It forces you to find your own way. I'm glad you talked about this
with him, and I hope you will share this letter with him as well. When I
come to visit, the three of us should have lunch together.

I understand the point your parishioner is making. There was a time,
in this country, when the pastor wrote the agenda for the church. He
(most of the clergy were male in those days) had to persuade the congregation to support that agenda, but it was clear that the vision of the congregation was no larger than the pastor's vision. In such congregations,
if a layperson wanted to institute a new idea, she had to convince the
pastor so that he could convince the congregation of its value. That
pretty much describes the church of my childhood. The power resided
in the person of the pastor.

Well into my ministry, I was shocked to discover that I was not the
most powerful member of the congregation. The only pastor I had ever
known was the pastor of my childhood. Any illusions that I could have
his kind of power were quickly dispelled. After I had expressed my

opinion, people voted the other way. If someone wanted to do something new in the church school, or with the building, or in the women's group, no one even thought of asking me. I remember complaining to Jackie and to friends about how hard it was to lead a church when I lacked the power to do so. I understand your retired pastor's viewpoint. A lot of active pastors are bitter and dispirited because the new generation of laypeople refuse to grant the pastor authority to carry out the responsibilities of the office.

Much has changed in our culture and in our churches. It's hard to find a church like the church of my childhood. A certain style of leadership fell victim to the Vietnam War. The powerful leader became the "enemy"—the president of the country, the general on the field, the dean of the university, the pastor of the parish. A whole generation of people, leaders today in this country and in the church, grew up with this lesson: never trust the leader; never trust those in power. Pastors and laypeople in our churches alike grew up afraid to lead, suspicious of power. Lay theologian William Stringfellow, writing in the 1970s, said:

> The most poignant victim of the demonic in America today is the so-called leader. . . . They are left with titles but without effectual authority; with the trappings of power, but without control over the institutions they head; in nominal command, but bereft of dominion.[1]

I agreed with Stringfellow when I first read those words. I think your parishioner still agrees. But Stringfellow's analysis doesn't ring true for us any longer—at least it doesn't for me. The title *pastor* no longer translates into institutional authority. Instead, that authority is spread among many leaders of the church. "Control" is not a good description of leadership in our time. Books on leadership describe a much more collegial understanding of power. And "dominion" is a term that is simply not in favor in our day. Pastors are not entitled to have dominion over congregations any more than humans are entitled to have dominion over the earth.

I have come to understand power in a new way. I believe the pastor is actually the most powerful figure in the congregation, and often in the community—but not in the old authoritative, controlling, "dominion" sense of the word *power*. You need to decide what kind of power you believe in, Lee. Is it the institutional power of my childhood pastor, or do you believe your power lies in your ability to empower the congregation? You need to make that choice soon.

Consider the plight of Frank. As an older clergyman, he understood his power as pastor to be the authority in the church. In the first months of his ministry he tried to persuade the Christian education committee to use the church-school curriculum of his choice, he ignored the deacons' preference for an order of worship, and he fired the treasurer. The previous pastor had tried to empower the congregation. With Frank, lay leaders felt they had been demoted from leaders to pawns. Within the first year a mutiny broke out. Key members who were the largest contributors to the church decided to leave. Frank had a real problem.

Most congregations would rebel against Frank's leadership. Even in the Roman Catholic Church, with its hierarchal ecclesiastical structure, a sense of empowerment prevails among the laity. I believe that is good. It is hard for most of us to adjust to this new leadership style, but it is good for the church and, given the post-Vietnam War culture of this country, we have no choice but to make the adjustment.

The point of this letter is to emphasize that in this new shared-leadership style, the pastor is still the most powerful figure in the congregation. Consider this passage from Paul's letter to the Philippians:

> Let the same mind be in you that was in Christ Jesus, who, though he was in the form of God, did not regard equality with God as something to be exploited, but emptied himself, taking the form of a slave, being born in human likeness. And being found in human form, he humbled himself and became obedient to the point of death—even death on a cross. Therefore God also highly exalted him and gave him the name that is above every name, so that at the name of Jesus every knee should bend, in heaven and on earth and under the earth, and every tongue should confess that Jesus Christ is Lord, to the glory of God the Father (Phil. 2:5-11).

Jesus, the powerful one, did not exploit his special relationship with God. Instead he emptied himself, took on the role of slave, humbled himself, and became obedient even to the point of death. Jesus became powerless. And the text says, "Therefore"—"*Therefore* God also highly exalted him . . ."

The power of the pastor is far greater than simply the power to endure. Real power resides in the stories, rituals, myths, and symbols that form the very foundation of the congregation. That is your power, Lee. Everything in the human experience can be found in the Scriptures—the best and the worst—and that is your text, week after week. As you handle those texts, as you pour out the water, as you hold up the loaf and cup, you connect the whole church to the power of the Holy Spirit. In your body, those symbols, stories, myths, and rituals are represented in the committee room, in the counseling session, in the community beyond the church. If you are steadfast in your refusal to claim your control, you will find power given to you.

The irony is that the church you are called to lead is often the agent of your own empowerment. Many times it is the congregation that leads the pastor. Fearfully, we hang back, not daring to take the needed risk. Courageously, congregational leaders put an arm around our shoulders and say, gently but firmly, "The time to act is now." That is not a condemnation of the pastor's timidity. It is a compliment. It points to the healthy and powerful congregational system the pastor has nurtured. The church baptized us and ordained us. Why should we be surprised when the church strengthens, leads, and empowers us?

My plea to you in this letter is to empower the church. When the power of the Spirit blows freely through the whole church, we pastors are not credited with great leadership skills. Something more wonderful happens: the power of the Spirit burns within all, even within us.

Your partner in building up the Body of Christ,

Paul

CHAPTER 6

The Wedding

June 30

Dear Lee,

Your first wedding, already! They sound like a great couple. Now you want to know how to proceed. Every wedding must be a terrific wedding. This is a point in the lives of the bridal couple and their parents at which real change is taking place. Knowing this is your first wedding, everyone will be eager to hear how you do. You must be a little nervous even now. I want to help you build a system that will guarantee success —well, 98 percent of the time.

Already you have been asked, and you will continue to be asked throughout your ministry, "Reverend, will you marry us?" What is your response to that question? What are your standards, your limits, and your values? You need to work out some answers for yourself and with your church board. Let me tell you what I have come to feel is right for me.

First, I ask myself the question, "Why not?" Some clergy will officiate only at weddings of people who are related to the congregation, since it represents the most time-consuming liturgical event in the ministry. These clergy feel it is not fair to the congregation to spend that much time on couples who simply like the architecture of the church building. I and the congregations I have served, however, believe that it is important to minister to the community. I see myself as a chaplain to the unchurched as well as pastor to the church, so I will marry those who are not affiliated with the congregation I serve. That's a little easier for me to say as one who is part of a large, multiple-staff church. You might find that position difficult, since you are the only pastor and Central

Church is one of the few Protestant churches in town. You could become overwhelmed. I am suggesting that you not decide against such ministry to the unaffiliated simply to protect your ministry to committed church members.

There may be other options. For instance, a retired minister in the area might be delighted to be asked to officiate at weddings. You could form a team, with the church's blessing. The retired pastor could at least take care of the counseling and the rehearsal; if the couple knew you and wanted you to "do" the wedding, you still could be included in the service. The honorarium could go to the retired pastor. Another solution would be to train a layperson to take over some of the planning and the rehearsal. Whatever you decide, I encourage you to find a way for the church to serve the community in this important ministry.

I also believe I do not have to judge whether a man and a woman are well suited for each other before agreeing to perform their wedding. After all, our incompatibilities are very often what make marriage so wonderful. But there are situations in which I will say no. If the bride and groom are members of another congregation in town and don't like their pastor, I won't proselytize. If they want me to conduct the service without mentioning God or Jesus Christ, I will suggest a justice of the peace or a Unitarian-Universalist colleague. If I am to be on vacation on the wedding date, I will usually say no. But I always try to recruit a minister to fill in for me—a colleague or a retired pastor. I never include my predecessor in that list, however. To do so could needlessly complicate both of our lives.

"Where will the wedding take place?" can be an important question, since some people do not want to use the church building but do want the benefit of your ministry. Couples come up with creative and unusual ideas these days—getting married in a park, or on a motorcycle. No answer is right for everyone, but you will find an answer that is right for you and for Central Church. That has to be clear, or you will be in trouble. A good friend of mine, who lives on the Boston Marathon route, married two runners in the midst of the race. He considered this an authentic act of ministry. I, on the other hand, would have felt that the setting was a circus environment.

The question gets harder. Will you share the wedding in a Roman Catholic parish down the street? Since you think of the Roman Catholic priest as a colleague and not a competitor, you will want to say yes. But you will want to talk with that priest to see what he thinks about such arrangements. Will you drive three hours each way on a Saturday to share in the service at the bride's church in Vermont? It depends on how close you are to this couple and how much time you have that weekend. Most couples are flexible. They will understand your point of view and respect your limitations if you explain your yes or no. In most cases when you say no, people will adjust their requests to accommodate your requirements.

A wedding brochure describing what the church offers and expects is helpful. The brochure will help those couples considering your church as one among many possibilities. It also makes plain that these expectations, policies, and fees are created not by you but by Central Church. I have enclosed a possible outline for such a publication [p. 36].

A wedding committee, an altar guild, or a wedding coordinator can be a great help to you. I have worked with all three in the churches I have served, and they made things run smoothly at both the rehearsal and the wedding. There are dozens of details I don't want to know anything about: flowers, bows, photographers, a needle and thread. No church is so small that it doesn't have at least one wonderful person who would love to help young couples with their weddings. If you have stated your policies clearly and a person or a committee is helping with logistics, you can focus your attention on the three areas where you are most needed: the counseling sessions, the rehearsal, and the wedding ceremony.

The *premarital counseling sessions* are crucial. They provide an opportunity to get to know one another, making the wedding a personal rather than an official event. At these sessions the couple plans the wedding. I give them a copy of the service in my denominational book of worship, a copy of the Roman Catholic liturgy, and orders of worship that others have used in this church. I also encourage them to look in a bookstore or library for other resources.[1] The liturgy needs to be theirs, not mine, but I explain that all three of us need to agree as to what is appropriate. Increasing numbers of couples want communion as part of their service; I remind them that everyone needs to be welcome at the table. Such family traditions as signing the family Bible or lighting candles make the wedding special and more personal.

I encourage the couple to include a sermon. It is never longer than five minutes, and it is given informally without notes, as an address to the bride and groom. This is a moment to get away from the formal liturgy, make a witness to the bridal couple, and help the congregation see this wedding as an occasion to renew their own family covenants. You need to have a couple of outlines in your file, but be careful to keep track of what you preached at which wedding. You don't want to use a sermon for another member of the same family.

"But," you ask, "what else should I do besides help them plan the liturgy? After all, these are premarital *counseling* meetings." Obviously, you need to start where the couple is. For many couples, this may be the first time they have met with a pastor on a personal level. If they grew up in the church, they probably saw the pastor as a distant figure in robes, or as a friend of their parents. More frequently, young people have never known a pastor and are scared to distraction of the first meeting. Your goal is to give them the experience of what you can do for them as a pastor. If they have problems, they can benefit from hearing a voice other than their own. If they have no problems, they can experience genuine pastoral affirmation.

Invariably, however, issues surface in planning the service. When the bride wants it one way but her mother wants it another way, you have an invitation to discuss family conflict with them. Many young couples are not clear whose wedding it is—theirs or their parents'—especially if the parents are paying the bill. Tension over the guest list is legendary and is a great opening to talk about in-law problems. I am convinced that if a young couple seems uncertain about their plans, everyone is ready to offer advice or directives. But if the couple is clear about what they want, the parents are more likely to say, "It will never work. But they love each other and will have to discover it for themselves."

When the couple can't agree, you have an invitation to explore how they deal with conflict . I grew up in a home where Mom and Dad never argued in front of the children. I assumed that married people didn't have conflict. Jackie showed me that some conflict can be creative. An honest conversation about handling conflict is helpful.

When one of them has trouble with traditional "God-talk" in the service, you have an opening to talk about faith, what it means to be married in a church rather than by a justice of the peace, the benefits of sharing in the life of a congregation as a couple. If they are not church members, I'm never shy about encouraging them to participate in a congregation.

The topic of sex in marriage will probably not come up spontaneously in the conversation. Increasing numbers of couples are sexually active or living together before marriage. Because Christians are deeply divided over changing moral standards on sexuality, these couples may assume that it is not safe to talk about their sexual experience with you. For other couples, sex is a taboo subject that is hard to discuss even with one another. You need to be clear how you yourself feel about these issues so that you can be open, candid, and free to talk about human sexuality with them. In my experience, sex and money are the topics most often argued about in marriages. We who counsel engaged couples do them no favor if we are afraid to talk about these issues. When I show my openness on these matters, I am often surprised at how many couples are looking for someone with whom they can discuss sexual issues and expectations. I always ask how they feel about becoming parents one day, since this is often the place in the conversation where issues of intimacy come to the surface.

I also initiate the topic of money management. The majority of couples in the suburban congregation I last served hadn't thought a moment about that subject. I suggested they needed to merge their separate incomes into one, with each person having some money of his or her own. I encourage couples to agree on a budget so that the one who manages the money won't be labeled as the one who controls the money. Many well-educated people have grown up with poor financial management skills. I think it is important to bring the subject to the surface before marriage begins.

My purpose is to demonstrate how a pastor can help the two of them come to a new frame of reference on their issues. If they seem to have significant problems, I urge them to find someone they trust to help before those problems spin out of control. But, most important, these meetings provide an opportunity for you to get to know this couple and for them to get to know you. When, years later, they ring you up to tell you what marriage has been like for them, you will know it was worth meeting with them again and again before the wedding.

The *wedding rehearsal* is the occasion when all your planning comes together. There is no room for democracy at the rehearsal. While the bride and groom have the right to change anything, you need to be a dictator at the wedding rehearsal. I watch the bridal couple's reactions carefully and encourage them to express their feelings. But no one else has any such rights. If a mother of the bride or a great aunt has an opinion, I respond courteously, defend the plans that the bride, the bridegroom, and I have worked out, and move on to the next instruction. This rehearsal is what makes the wedding "fun" for everyone. People will enjoy themselves more if they know what they are to do, where they are to stand, and why. I tell everyone at the start, "This rehearsal means you won't be nervous tomorrow—guaranteed. If anyone is nervous, see the wedding coordinator."

Finally, the rehearsal *must* be over in one hour. In that time frame, here is what has to be done. The wedding party has to know where to stand and how to get there. The ushers need to learn how to get the congregation, along with families of the bride and groom, in and out of the church. If there is a receiving line at church, you need to help the couple decide who will be in the line and where each will stand. At your last counseling meeting, ask the couple to bring three things to the rehearsal: the wedding license, fees to be kept until the wedding, and an answer to the question, "How many pews shall we save for relatives?" I have enclosed a sample schedule for the rehearsal along with this letter [pp. 37-38].

Despite all my bravado at the rehearsal, everyone is nervous on the big day. Someone has to be calm—and you are elected. Pretend at least. Every wedding has an emergency. Be prepared to help people respond. At one wedding the bride fainted in my arms; as we carried her out the side door, I poked my head back to say, "We'll be right back; enjoy the organ music. Don't go away." A few moments with her head between her knees brought her back, and she marched in confidently; the congregation came through with a standing ovation (with the help of a few gestures from me). At another ceremony, when the bridesmaid read 1 Chronicles 13 instead of 1 Corinthians 13, I searched desperately for a way to tie that text to the sermon. Finding none, I simply went on with a straight face. No one seemed to notice, but I learned always to have the text read at the rehearsal. Yet another time the bride was 20 minutes late, and the organist had to play the same piece three times. I finally made the following announcement: "Ladies and Gentlemen, the bride is delayed. Won't you all feel free to get up, stroll in the garden, enjoy the sunshine. When we are ready, the church bell will sound." When the bride eventually arrived, she was furious that everyone wasn't sitting in place waiting for her. But the organist felt that justice had been done, and the congregation was relieved. My point? Keep your cool.

The wedding reception is the most trying event of all for me. Often I know only the bride and groom. Many clergy simply never attend. I have always felt that policy to be a little too impersonal. You and Chris will be invited to all wedding receptions, and you will need to decide how to handle these invitations. This is how Jackie and I decide whether to accept: I make a point of being there for the grace at least, but I don't always stay the whole time. Jackie comes to the wedding and reception only if we know the couple well enough to give them a wedding gift.

You can see that each wedding consumes hours of your time. The good news is that in the process, a real bond can develop between the bridal couple and the pastor. May you be blessed with that friendship often, Lee.

Yours in the joy of the wedding feast,

Paul

An Outline for a Wedding Brochure

• **Welcome**

Enthusiastically welcome couples who approach you for assistance. But also state clearly your basic policy on whether nonmembers are welcome to use the church building and your clergy services for their wedding.   .

• **Procedures**

— Encourage couples to set the date of the wedding and the rehearsal as far ahead as possible.
— State the number of premarital counseling meetings that you require. Encourage the bride and groom to arrange for the first meeting soon.
— The couple must arrange to meet with the organist to plan the music; the church office will inform the organist when the date is set.
— Explain the role of the wedding committee. A member will contact the couple.
— State your policy on receptions held in the church, including whether alcoholic beverages are allowed in the building.
— Explain the marriage-license requirements of the state.
— Outline the rules for the wedding itself. For instance, is photography, with or without flash, or videotaping allowed during the service? What about throwing rice? What is the smoking policy?
— List the names, addresses, and phone numbers of the staff— clergy, secretary, organist, sexton.

• **Fee Schedule for Clergy, Organist, and Sexton**

You may wish to set a different fee schedule for church members, on the assumption that they have already paid the clergy and contributed to the maintenance and utilities of the building. The official board should set the fee schedules. I urge setting a generous fee for the organist and insisting that he or she be present at the rehearsal. Many couples ride away from the church in a limousine. I don't think they should be stingy with the church staff.

A Sample Schedule for a Wedding Rehearsal

1. Welcome

Do this at the front of the church. This is a time to state the purpose of the rehearsal and help put people at ease. A brief prayer or meditation may help focus the participants.

2. Wedding Service Walk-through

- Don't start with the processional, because the participants won't know where to go when they get to the front of the church. Start with the wedding itself. Arrange everyone at the front of the church so they are standing or sitting where they will be at the wedding. The bride will figure out who will go out with whom and how that affects the arrangement of attendants.

- **Walk through the service.**
  - Don't read every word, but describe the elements.
  - If there is movement, act it out. Walk up to the altar and back. Pay attention to details. For instance, if the bride has a train, she will need someone to help her back up or turn around. If the father of the bride needs to sit down with his wife as soon as he and the bride arrive at the front of the church, he needs to be on the bride's left so that he doesn't have to jump over her train.
  - If participants from the congregation have a part, have them walk through it. At some time in the rehearsal have them read their parts with the speaker system on.

3. Recessional and Processional

- At the end of the service walk-through, practice the *recessional* with music.
- With everyone at the back of the church, organize for the *processional*. Practice the processional with the music.
- Ask if anyone wants to practice any part of the service again. Usually there is a "yes" from someone. Walk through the service again, and practice departing and entering again.
- Ask again if there are questions about the service itself.

- Remind everyone of the time of the service and the time they need to be at the church.
- Let the musicians leave if they are not attending any subsequent rehearsal dinner.

4. Instructions to Ushers

- Gather the ushers at the front of the church; make sure the couple is nearby to answer questions.
- Explain how to usher family members in.
- Explain seating arrangements, including the reserved places for relatives. While Emily Post's etiquette would have the friends of the bride sit on the left of the altar and friends of the groom on the right, most couples will keep the relatives in that arrangement but mix the congregation together.
- Ask the ushers to enforce any photo, rice, or smoking prohibitions.
- Explain how to start the wedding (usher in parents of groom, then mother of bride).
- Explain how to usher people out (parents of bride, parents of groom, grandparents, the congregation by pew).
- Show where everyone should go after the recessional.

5. Arrival Time and Place

Depending on what arrangements you have made about prewedding preparations, I would follow these basic guidelines:

- The wedding should start on time.
- Bride's attendants should arrive 20 minutes before the wedding.
- Ushers should arrive 45 minutes before the wedding.
- The groom and groomsmen can wait in the pastor's office, beginning 20 minutes before the wedding.
- Make arrangements for the reception line if it is to be at the church.
- Ask one last time if there are questions about anything.

Exactly one hour after beginning the rehearsal, you will say: "See you tomorrow!"

CHAPTER 7

The Funeral

July 8

Dear Lee,

In each congregation I have served, I was faced, within a week of my
arrival, with the funeral of a significant church member. While I was
nervous each time, in retrospect I think it helped me establish my pastoral authority quickly. The congregation saw that I was able not only
to manage the situation but also to capture the essence of the deceased.
Now you too have the funeral of a significant church member within
weeks of your moving to town. I am sending this letter by e-mail so that
it might help in planning this first funeral.

Culture shapes our funeral customs. When we try to oppose culture,
we usually lose. All sorts of family history and customs will influence
the decisions people make about funerals for their loved ones. In one
sense, the first week after a family member dies is not a teachable moment. This is not the time to insist on a new liturgy or to argue for a different attitude toward death. We need to teach people about issues of
death and dying long before they experience grief. Much of the material
in this letter needs to be shared with people in the context of continuing
education, not when the funeral is the day after tomorrow. Having said
that, I would add that many people are forever grateful for a suggestion
that is fresh and new, even in the terrible days of raw sorrow. The long
journey through grief is different for each person. I am simply urging
compassion, patience, and the understanding that the way we say good-
bye is different for each of us.

If at a retreat you asked, "When did you experience God present in your life?" probably 85 percent of the answers would link the holy, sacred moment with the death of a loved one. Even the Bible witnesses to this truth: "In the year that King Uzziah died I saw the Lord sitting upon a throne, high and lifted up" (Isa. 6:1, RSV). More than a cultural moment, death is a holy moment. We who serve God must respect the dying and the grieving. Drop everything and get yourself there when word comes of death, even if it is your day off. That may not be the moment to teach people about funeral customs, but it is the moment to sensitize people to the presence of God. You will often be startled by the discovery that God is there for you as well.

Are there any good reasons why you should refuse to conduct a funeral? If no one in the family is a church member or a Christian? If the deceased was a scoundrel? None of that means you should refuse to officiate at the funeral, in my opinion. I have always told the funeral director that I was willing to conduct anyone's funeral, even if there was no money for an honorarium. Leading the funeral for an unchurched family isn't as difficult a decision as a wedding. The time commitment is far less for a funeral than for a wedding. Also, the whole church can share in the ministry to the grieving family in a way that all members cannot share in the preparation of the bride and groom for the wedding. But in some cases you might still want to arrange with a retired pastor to help. Again, I believe that you should not invite your predecessor to assist with weddings and funerals. It isn't fair to one who wants to retire, and it isn't fair to you, who need to prove you are capable of serving people in their joy and sorrow.

Why not conduct the funeral? The two hard-and-fast rules are these. First, I will not conduct the service of a person who was a member of my former congregation. I will attend but not officiate or share in the service. My successor needs to do that. Second, I will not conduct the funeral if the family is a member of another congregation, unless the pastor of that church has asked me to share it, or to conduct it in his or her absence.

Some issues will come up continually. You and the church board need to be of one mind on them. Where should the funeral be—at the funeral home, at the home of the deceased, or at the church? I encourage people who are Christians to have the service in the church, but I will hold the service at any of the locations mentioned. I also encourage people to close the casket during the worship service so that the focus can be on life. But I will not refuse to do the service if the casket is open. Finally, I encourage people who are planning a cemetery committal service out of state to find a pastor near that cemetery to preside at the committal (I try to supply names if that is helpful). But on occasion I will go.

Let me speak with you about the funeral director, Lee. We clergy have been hard on "undertakers." They have to make a living. When we expect them to tell families that "the pastor doesn't like open caskets," when we want them to arrange funerals so that they will not interrupt our day off, when we encourage our people not to allow the funeral director to be present at the church service, when we imply that funeral directors exploit the grieving—that's unfair, unjust, and untrue. Pastors who do that—and there are many—are themselves the losers. I have always had excellent working relationships with funeral directors. They have gone out of their way to help me, and I have done the same for them.

So how do you deal with a death in the congregation? First, I visit the family. The purpose of the first visit, as close to the time of death as possible, is to connect with the grief. I try not to talk about the funeral except to set the time. In a separate visit, either in the home or in my office, whichever suits the family, we plan the funeral together. The more family members present, the better. I have with me a printout of an order of worship, a hymnal, and a pad of paper. I listen to what they want in the service. My purpose is to do it their way. This is not the place to criticize their taste in music or poetry. We do talk about the problems. If, for example, they want a 15-minute service and four of them want to speak and they want five hymns, I point out the problem. But I try to figure out how to make it work. When their ideas are out in the open, I pass out copies of the order of worship and show where and how it will accommodate their desires. With computer technology we can easily produce an order of worship that reflects those decisions. I leave this printout with them, along with the hymnal, and encourage them to make changes in prayers and to select hymns and Scripture readings.

After we have discussed the order of worship, with my pad of paper before me, I ask family members to tell me about this one whom they have lost. I encourage them to supply anecdotes rather than adjectives. For me to say, "He was a good father," is fine, but it is far more effective if they can tell me a story demonstrating that truth. I simply take notes. It's a redemptive process for the family. Usually stories pour out along with tears.

The family must make the basic decision whether to have a funeral or a memorial service. At the funeral, the coffin with the body is present. If this is the local or family custom, remember how hard it is to change the culture of burial customs. There are good theological reasons for having it this way. It avoids dualism, separation between body and spirit. Memorial services often follow cremations, graveside services, or the burial of the body at a distant location. There are good theological reasons for these services as well. They keep our attention focused on the God who gave life, not on the remains or the beauty of the casket. I like to do the cemetery committal service before the memorial service. That brief worship at graveside is the hardest of all for a family, however. It really is "good-bye."

Remember that this funeral or memorial service is a celebration of life. The death may have been tragic, your eyes may be filled with tears, but my point stands: the funeral is as much a celebration of life and love as the wedding. Once you have incorporated this truth into your soul, the rest comes naturally.

Preparing the service for one of the saints is never hard, but it's tough if the deceased was a scoundrel. Ultimately, it's a matter of organizing the blessed stories and memories into a cohesive witness. I try to be as courageous as possible. If this beloved saint drove everyone crazy with her long-winded stories, I say something like, "She's bending God's ear there in heaven as we speak." The more honest we can be about a weakness, the more believable our description of integrity. If the family couldn't stand the "beloved departed," I deal with the guilt that is a part of grief, or if they give me permission, I confront the problems of family life. If there was a suicide, I all but insist that we be honest about how this death occurred. In my experience, courage pays off. People want to be personal at a funeral, and honesty is a gift if it is possible. The prayers are another element in which you can add this personal touch.

In most churches these days simple refreshments are served following the worship. It's a wonderful time when people can add their stories. Since the service or the committal may have been very painful, it makes sense to follow that with a celebration of God's grace. But remember, if the family goes to the cemetery, the congregation won't wait for them to return to the church, and I don't think it is fair to ask the funeral director to wait around for the coffee hour to end before going with you to the burial site.

Follow-up visits with the family are crucial. Within a week, after the relatives and friends have left, you need to be there. I have a file that reminds me to visit once a month for six months. I also visit on the anniversary of the death and on holidays, if possible.

Every service is different. Sometimes the deceased will be a stranger, and you will have to struggle to avoid just going through the motions. At other times you will bury a close friend, and you will struggle to hold yourself together until after the benediction. By the way, if you don't hold yourself together, if you start to cry in the middle of the sermon, don't be ashamed of your tears. Hard as it is for you to speak through your tears, it is often easier for others to hear through them. Through it all, remember that these moments of grief, as when King Uzziah died, are holy indeed.

Yours in wonder and awe before life and death,

Paul

CHAPTER 8

The Baptism

July 15

Dear Lee,

I know it seems that everyone is ganging up on you with weddings, funerals, and baptisms. The funerals come unexpectedly, and the weddings have been in the planning stages for months. But with baptisms, it may well be true. People probably *have* been waiting for the new pastor to baptize their child. Expect a lot of these services in the first months of your ministry in a new church.

On more than one occasion I have had a parent ask me, "Reverend, will you do my baby?" I have always wanted to respond, "Rare, medium, or well done?" I have never succumbed to that bit of levity, however, because I always work hard to help people understand that baptism is central to the life of the church. It is the occasion when the couple promises to bring the child up in the Christian faith. It is also the occasion when the church promises to support the parents and the child in that covenant. In a real sense the entire church program, including the church school, youth programs, and confirmation flow directly from this baptismal vow of the congregation. Indeed, the whole of our Christian life is a reaffirmation of baptism. This sacrament is at the center of the faith.

Since many congregations and most church members think baptism is a name-giving ritual (christening), we have to work hard to reclaim this sacrament. Here are three teaching opportunities I have used.

First, this is a chance to explore the matter of trinitarian language. Inclusive language is an issue for at least half of the people in our denominational tradition who bring children for baptism. Strong emotion is voiced on both sides of the issue. Those who want the traditional language, "I baptize you in the name of the Father, the Son, and the Holy Spirit," claim the Trinity as the universal mark of the faith. They believe that a change in these words would break covenant with the ecumenical church. If a child is baptized with other words, will that baptism be recognized in the wider church? Those who want to use a gender-inclusive trinitarian formula insist that God is not male and that our language needs to reflect that theological truth. Liturgical scholar Ruth Duck, in *Gender and the Name Of God: The Trinitarian Baptismal Formula*, describes some alternatives.[1] Two of these I find appealing. One, "I baptize you in the name of Jesus Christ," was, according to Duck, "accepted in the Roman Catholic Church until at least the thirteenth century."[2] The other, used at Riverside Church in Manhattan, is "I baptize you in the name of the Father and the Son and the Holy Spirit, One God, Mother of us all."[3] What is really important to me, however, is not whether we should insist on the traditional formula, use an alternative, or give each family a choice. Rather, I care about the educational process that makes the sacrament precious in the minds and hearts of the congregation. I want to urge you to engage the church in this question. It forces people to look at the meaning of the Trinity and the meaning of baptism.

Second, the home visit is crucial. It is an occasion to talk about the family system, the effect this new child has on everyone. It is also a moment when questions about the Christian faith are urgent. Seldom is this a superficial visit. Make sure to schedule it when significant conversation is possible.

Your third teaching opportunity related to baptism is reflected in the question, "How old do you have to be to receive communion?" One of the congregations I served spent a wonderful year considering that question. The debate was between those who would require confirmation before a child could receive communion and those who claim it as a family meal to which all the baptized are welcome. As soon as someone said, "Little children don't know enough about communion to receive it," the adults had to admit they didn't know much either. They were ready for an adult-education program on the sacraments. At the same time, the Christian educators had to write a curriculum for children on the sacraments so that they would be prepared for the bread and the cup. It was a great year in which both communion and baptism became more significant for all.

Some of your people may come from traditions that observe believer's baptism. In our tradition, one is baptized as an infant and confirmed as a youth or adult. In other traditions, infants are dedicated; one is baptized as a youth or adult. This letter on baptism is relevant in regard to both the infant who is baptized and the infant who is dedicated.

Are there any reasons you should not baptize a child? Again, guidelines should be reviewed with your church board. If parents promise to bring up children in the Christian faith, does at least one of those parents need to be a church member? I have always felt a little uncomfortable with such a stance. It is like saying, "You have to belong to the club before I will baptize your child." Does one parent need to be baptized? Will parents engage in adult education so that they will know more about the faith they are promising to pass on? For me, the important thing is to challenge parents to deepen their faith as they promise to pass it on. Commitment is required here. We can't be haphazard. But I don't believe it is the pastor's place to decide if the commitment and intention to be a part of the church community are adequate. The challenge should be put clearly to the parents, and it is up to them to decide whether to proceed with the baptism or to wait until the child is of confirmation age.

More complex is this question: Will you baptize in your church the child of a couple whom you married but who now live elsewhere? Of course they want you to do the baptism, and of course you want to do it as well. But they need to get involved in a church where they live. This moment could motivate them to do so. If you agree to baptize the child, you may take that moment away. You may feel pressured to do it, especially by grandparents who are active in your congregation. You need at least to confront the family with the issue. More often than not they will say, "You're right. We'll have the child baptized at a church near home." A colleague I respect says in these situations, "I'll do this one, but not the next."

As you know, in our tradition the baptism occurs in the course of the worship service. Will you hold a private baptismal service for family only? Many colleagues say no: One has to be in the midst of the congregation for the church's promise to mean anything. Many couples, however, come from churches where baptism is always private, so I will observe that tradition and bring a deacon along to make the promise on the church's behalf. I have never baptized a child in the swimming pool or at the beach. When people who suggest such a setting are helped to understand the connection between the church and baptism, they usually go along, though sometimes grudgingly.

Large congregations often have a tradition of scheduling baptisms three or four times a year. I have always been open to any date, so long as it doesn't conflict with another event, making the service too long. Baptisms often need to be scheduled when the extended family is going to gather from out of town. That's fine; we're talking about a sacrament of grace, after all. When too many rules are associated with baptism, something important is lost. Besides, it's good for the congregation to celebrate baptism frequently. It puts children front and center, reminds us of the importance of passing on the faith to the next generation, and gives all worshipers the opportunity to renew their own baptismal covenants.

So how do you do it? You will need to develop your own style. I try to follow the following guidelines. First, I find a liturgy that is more tactile than verbal. There should be some evidence that the water is real. Let folk hear it being poured from pitcher to font. Make sure the water is warm. Icy water on a bald head makes infants and old men scream!

I take the child in my arms. One day a young, single colleague performing his first baptism took the child in both arms and then tried to figure out how to get a hand free to dip into the water. It had be one of the funniest baptisms in history. You may want to experiment with babies before getting to the baptismal font. If the child is screaming and holding onto the parent for dear life, of course, don't try to take the child away.

I try to memorize the service. Holding an infant in my arms and reading from a service book seems inauthentic to me. Pay attention to your feelings. Often the parents are nervous, and their jitters are conveyed to the child. If you are calm, everyone will feel better. During the hymn following the baptism, I carry the child with me into the congregation, assuming the child and parents are comfortable with that.

You may find that several older children in the congregation have not been baptized. You can wait until confirmation to baptize them or arrange to have several baptized together so that no one feels too awkward. In our congregation adult baptisms usually occur during the service that welcomes new members into the church.

Well, Lee, you see from these last three letters that the wedding, funeral, and baptism are central to your ministry and not impossible to perform. In my June 30 letter I spoke of a system that will guarantee success. If you experience any difficulty with that guarantee, call my wedding coordinator. She's used to complaining people!

In tears and gladness, I remain your grateful partner,

Paul

CHAPTER 9

Planning for Sunday

July 23

Dear Lee,

This is the season I am usually preparing the "Sunday Plan" for next year—you remember that document that everyone teased me about when you were a seminarian with us. To my knowledge, of all the seminarians I have worked with over the past 25 years, only two actually follow my example and create a sermon plan for the year. I hope you'll be the third. I've enclosed a sample of the chart I use to map out the year [p. 57].

Let me start by identifying some assumptions and asking some basic questions.

- How often have you heard jokes about ministers working only one hour a week? Behind that attempt at humor is this fact: Sunday morning is the time when everyone notices you; therefore, quite bluntly, you had better do a good job. I have known clergy who have, in fact, not done much else and, because they were terrific worship leaders, they got along just fine. Not only will your current congregation judge you by your Sunday "performance," but every future search committee will do the same. You may think that is a cynical viewpoint. To be honest, however, I found that the quality of public worship was at the top of the list of what Jackie and I wanted whenever we were looking for a church to join.

- Who is in charge of worship? One problem is that often no one is leading worship at all; rather, a half-dozen people are doing their own thing. That lack of leadership will be blatantly clear to all who sit in the pew. When the sermon talks about grace and the anthem is about judgment and the children's sermon focuses on nature, everyone knows that no one is in charge. The preacher is the leader of worship. That needs to be made clear to clergy and laity alike. Whoever preaches the sermon on any Sunday also leads the whole worship service. If I, as senior minister, have a great idea for a liturgical reading, I must get permission if my associate is preaching.

- That does not mean the preacher gets all the credit or the blame. The old authoritarian style was to make sure only the senior minister's ego was satisfied. Under those conditions, no organist should stand out, no soloist should get praise, no storyteller should expect a compliment at the door. Moreover, the senior minister would read and approve the associate's sermon before it was delivered—hardly a collegial act. The authoritarian preacher took the blame for any act of bad judgment on anyone's part. The assumption I promote is that each participant takes credit or blame. If everyone suffered through the anthem, and people complain to me about it, I tell them to speak to the choir director directly. If everyone loved the anthem, we need to compliment both the choir and the director. I believe good leadership ensures that everyone is affirmed who deserves affirmation.

- Will you follow the lectionary? There are good reasons to be critical of the ecumenical lectionary. The Hebrew Scriptures are handled tenuously or used as proof texts for the Gospel reading. I find it shocking that the book of Job is never considered in its entirety. The readings often end at awkward points, sometimes just before the main point of the biblical text. Nevertheless, I follow the lectionary because it is good for me and for the congregation. It links us ecumenically, it disciplines the preacher, and, with a lectionary-based curriculum, adults and children can consider a common biblical topic. I'm not a slave to the prescribed readings, however. I will often put a topical sermon in here or a sermon series in there. But generally people can expect to hear a sermon based on the day's appointed lectionary readings.

- What is the liturgy? How does it relate to the sermon? I believe that each worship service is held together by a theme. The readings, music, prayers, children's time, and sermon all ought to relate to one another. The sermon is not the main feature. It is part of the whole.

How do you plan worship? The answer is the same whether you plan by the year or by the season: You need to plan ahead. If the preacher comes up with a sermon idea on Wednesday morning, then the anthem, which the choir has already been rehearsing for three weeks, will almost certainly not fit into the preacher's theme. Regardless of who leads the children's sermon, the Christian-education people need to be ready to help children respond to it. The altar guild needs to know when there is to be a baptism, communion, or a change in liturgical seasons. The secretary needs to include the sermon title and biblical text in the church newsletter and in the local newspaper; the sexton needs to arrange the baptismal font; the musicians need to know what special events are planned so they can decide when the choir can be scheduled to sing a very long anthem.

Staff meetings can be the best occasions for planning worship, since most of those who will participate in the worship attend those meetings. For example, in early November we go through the plan for Advent and Christmas. We pick the hymns so that "Joy to the World" isn't sung three Sundays in a row; we decide on liturgical dance; we schedule the children's times. Everyone is clear by mid-November on the plans for the Advent and Christmas services, and everyone has had a part in the planning.

Obviously, if that is to happen, the preacher needs to have done some homework before the staff meeting. The Sunday plan I have enclosed is that homework [p. 57]. There you will find a plan for text, sermon title, worship theme, and special events such as baptism, communion, children to receive Bibles, and so forth. How does the preacher make that plan? First, settle with colleagues and deacons who will preach when. I believe that is best done *with* colleagues, not *for* them. Include guest preachers in that list. All of this needs to be done in the summer if the Sunday plan is to function for the following program year, September to August.

In the summer, choose the themes for the Sundays. Here is how I do it: I make a list of ideas I'd like to use based on the reading I have done through the year; I study the lectionary; I sit down for a day or more and write down what I think we as a church need to focus on in worship. With all of that paper spread out on the table, it's easy to write the schedule. I share that draft with all involved in the worship, as well as with the deacons, the council, and anyone else who wants a copy.

Don't let special services that do not fall on Sundays (such as Christmas Eve, Ash Wednesday, Maundy Thursday, Good Friday, the Easter Vigil, a vesper service) get lost in the shuffle. They are as important as Sunday morning and take just as much planning.

Consider the matter of innovative worship. When innovation is done well, worship is a powerful experience. For example, at one church I served we always held the Maundy Thursday Service of the Tenebrae in the sanctuary. A faithful few always came and said it was one of the most meaningful events of the year. One year we decided to move it out of the sanctuary and into the fellowship hall. The idea was that the simple fish chowder and bread would be communion; after the meal, right there at the tables, the events of the "night Jesus was betrayed" would be read by several deacons, each of whom would take the part of one person in the story. Whole families came; the children were filled with awe. When the lights were all extinguished, 200 of us sat around tables in the stillness. God was there. I knew it, as did everyone else in the room.

Another example: One Easter Sunday, which was also a communion Sunday, the Gospel lesson was John's story of the risen Christ cooking fish by the sea at dawn. We gave each of the thousand worshipers bread, wine, and fish—salmon caught by a member of the parish. Years later people commented on that Easter service when we served fish along with the bread and wine and remembered Christ's call to Peter and to us: "Follow me."

Innovation not only can build community within your congregation, it can build relations between churches as well. One summer a group of congregations came together for common worship rather than each church worshiping in its own building. Held outdoors at a park by the sea and followed by a picnic, the service became a tradition that reminded us all that we are sisters and brothers, not competitors.

If innovative worship is to work, it needs to be planned with the following realities in mind:

- It needs to make sense. You need to be able to explain why you want to serve fish to a thousand people—to make the text come to mind every time we receive the sacrament.

- No one should be surprised. Tell people again and again if worship is being moved from the sanctuary to the park for one Sunday in the summer. You can promote this event in several ways to appeal to different people: as an ecumenical Sunday, as an ecological Sunday, and as a family Sunday. People need to be told why you are doing it, what to wear, and what to bring. Innovation must be planned months in advance.

- The new feature must be accompanied by a generous helping of the familiar. The Tenebrae service I mentioned was the same liturgy that had been used in the sanctuary— the location and the meal were the only new elements. People need the familiar along with the new.

- Be sensitive to the preferences you know exist in the congregation. The longer you are there, the easier it will be to know how far you can depart from tradition. If you know an innovation is going to drive a certain parishioner crazy, talk with her ahead of time and encourage her to come with an open mind.

- Innovative worship is four times the work of a traditional worship service. The systems are all in place for the worship we do Sunday after Sunday. Ushers know where to get the offering plates; the altar guild knows where the plates and cups go; the liturgist knows where the Bible is going to be and how the speaker system works. Move to a park, and you have to rethink all those details. If one of these "little things" is forgotten, the whole event is at risk.

How do you develop each service? Remember, worship is not something you create and give to the congregation; it is something the congregation creates with you. The visits you made last week, the counseling you did yesterday, the clergy association meeting you attended two weeks ago—all these feed the worship. There are ways to structure community creativity. Clergy discussion groups that gather for Bible study can provide creative help for those preaching on a common lectionary text. A good mix of denominations and traditions enriches the process. Or gather a Bible study group in the congregation with the understanding that a sermon will grow out of your discussion of the lectionary text. You may find that this approach wears thin after a season, but it is a good thing to do now and then. Or discuss the texts at your staff meeting and with key lay folk who might have something to offer.

That communal practice leads into your own creative process. I begin with a study of the materials (usually on Tuesday). I study the text, read the commentaries, and reread what my favorite scholars have written on the theme. As ideas occur to me during the year, I toss them into a shoe box, so I look in there next. (I know that it would be better to enter these insights into the computer, and I will learn to do that one day soon!) On Wednesday I "put myself into the text" and try to imagine what it was like for the writer and those for and about whom he was writing. I consider how the congregation might respond to the text, and, using the work from the day before, I try to get a clear purpose in mind. If the theme reads like a term paper, I realize more work is needed. If it seems too predictable, it needs much more work. I like to end the day with an outline that is detailed enough to allow me to write the sermon in a couple of hours on Thursday. Others prefer to write a draft that can be drastically edited the next day.

On Friday I try to get the whole worship service carefully planned. I spend time on preparing the words of the call to worship, the introduction to the offering, and the prayers. Also on Friday, I prepare the material I will need on Sunday: I mark the pages to be used in the hymnal with paper clips, and I print out a large-print copy of the sermon manuscript and liturgy. When I am not using a manuscript, I create a preaching outline with key phrases written down. By the time I have worked and reworked it that much, it is almost memorized. I then put it in the drawer and have a good day off on Saturday.

Before worship on Sunday I read the manuscript and then preach it to myself to make sure I don't have to be tied too closely to the script or outline. I rehearse the announcements, since that is where I am most apt to stutter and stammer. Then comes the most important preparation. You've seen track-and-field competitors run the race in their mind. I do that with the service. I imagine every detail—stand/sit, microphone on/off, move from pulpit to table. Finally, remember this: Catastrophes occur regularly, and the test of a good worship leader is the ability to recover from mistakes with grace and humor. A great pastor can turn an error into a fine illustration of the point. Therefore, your last step is to forget your memorized phrases and focus on the point you hope to make one way or another. Then I am ready for the prayer with the other worship participants.

Let me mention three habits that I think are important:

1. Inclusive language is a given these days.

Young families are not going to stay with you if you say "mankind" instead of "humankind." I know this language is second nature to you now, Lee. God is not a macho patriarch in your mind, so God doesn't come across as a male in your speaking.

2. The pace of worship is not so easily learned.

Worship becomes boring when it drags, when everyone knows what you are about to say, when people are expected to watch with fascination as you make your way from pulpit to altar. You don't need to announce anything, including hymns, that is printed in the order of worship. Be where you need to be exactly when you need to speak from that spot. Keep everything—including the sermon—moving.

3. Remember that even when you are not speaking, you are still leading worship.

I worked with an associate once who made last-minute corrections on the sermon manuscript during the Scripture reading. That is not acceptable. Be an attentive participant throughout.

Evaluation is the most important part of your work as a worship leader. Your fans will always say, "Wonderful sermon, Pastor," but don't rely on their evaluation. Pay attention to the people who usually tell you the truth. Reach out to one of them, especially if you noticed them staring at their feet during worship, and ask what they thought. Now and then, a sermon discussion time is a good exercise, especially if you have brought up controversial issues. You need to hear both the praise and the constructive criticism. It is hard to listen to criticisms of your sermon, but that feedback is one of the most helpful things a congregation can give you. Even if you are hurt, don't show it. If you do, you'll never get an honest comment from that parishioner again. Write down the critical comment, put it aside for a few days, and when you are ready to consider it, take it out and think it over. Remember, most criticisms are meant to be helpful, not hurtful.

Are you feeling a little overwhelmed by how much work goes into worship leadership? I hope so! Those who wing it with worship preparation always insult the act of worship itself. Pastoral ministry is hard work. It would take more than an hour a week even if worship were all you did. No one needs to know how long it takes. Worshipers simply need to discover to their surprise at the end of the hour that they actually did worship God.

Your colleague in praise,

Paul

The Sunday Plan 19___ to 19___

Date Liturgical Color	Parish Event	Sermon Title Text	Central Idea	Children's Time
Sept. 3 Green	Communion Labor Day weekend	Lay sermon by (name of preacher)		
Sept. 10 Green	Brunch Commission church-school teachers and youth advisors	**A Family Challenge** Luke 14: 25-33	Jesus challenged the family system of his day, and our day too.	Title and person in charge of children's time

CHAPTER 10

Making Christian Education Work

July 31

Dear Lee,

I'm sure that both you and the church-school teachers are getting a little nervous. You asked me, "How do I make the Christian education program work?" Since you have just started, you will have to make do with some shortcuts this first year. So I will answer from the larger perspective.

Christian education is the central work of the church. The trustees, the deacons, and every church committee must take part in educating the congregation. Growing in faith and passing the faith on from one generation to another is the mission of Christian education.

The trouble is, nostalgia rules in the church, especially in the church school. By and large, the experience people had as children defines their educational goals for today's church. Since life has changed in the last generation, the Christian education program requires leadership that can move it in new directions. Here are some of the principles that have changed since I was a child:

- Christian education is for the whole church, not just for the children.
- Christian nurture occurs everywhere, not just in the church school.
- Everyone shares the teaching task, not just Sunday school teachers.
- With a diverse membership, everyone has something to learn and teach.

Many churches assume that people learn everything they need to know before they join the church. The confirmation program and the new-membership classes are expected to perform miracles. I believe we join the church in order to learn. Like the disciples, we are meant to be lifelong learners. The classes that prepare us for membership acquaint us with the culture of the church universal, our unique tradition, and this particular congregation. This is a particularly important function in a time when many adults join the church without any religious education. Many have never been inside a church, except to attend a wedding or a funeral. They need an orientation to survive. When a child comes from a foreign country to attend public school in the United States, she needs immediate help with the language, the classroom routine, the way she is expected to dress and behave. Acculturation to the church is no less urgent.

But the real learning occurs after the church members have a sense of truly belonging. When a child is baptized, the whole church promises to share in that child's nurture in the faith. When adults join the church, the whole congregation promises to walk with them in fellowship and love. These rites of the church are occasions when we all promise to teach and learn from one another. So everyone is a part of the education program, whether he teaches in a classroom every Sunday morning, greets a child by name in the coffee hour, or offers a new family a ride to worship. Witness is the way we teach and learn.

So how do you manage the process of getting the church school running by the second Sunday in September? *Leadership is the key.* Over the past 20 years far fewer people have entered degree programs to become Christian education directors. This decrease is due in part to the fact that many potential Christian education specialists were women who found opportunities for pastoral ministry opening up to them in ways previously impossible. Also, in a time of shrinking church membership, the Christian education person was often the first to go when staff cuts were made. As the job opportunities became less attractive, seminaries were forced to cut back their Christian education degree programs. Most educators in the church today are laypeople who have found nondegree educational opportunities. Consequently, excellent leadership is now available for both small and large churches. Wonderful training resources can also help you or people in the congregation provide the necessary leadership. Either way, quality leadership in the Christian education program is essential. Here's how I recommend you proceed.

1. As pastor, you need to lead the educational program of the church.

The congregation will discern your commitment or lack of interest. Many people join a congregation that they believe will nurture their children in the faith. Failing in this key area could be disastrous for your church. Therefore, it is imperative that you respect the educational program, show gratitude for teachers, insist that the spaces where children and adults learn be of equal quality (would adults be happy meeting in the boiler room, as my church-school class did when I was a child?), include children in the worship service, and involve yourself as a teacher and as a resource for other teachers.

2. You need the help of people who will focus on this program of the church and provide the hands-on leadership.

This leadership requires two qualities: (1) a clear and broad vision of what might be and (2) the ability to give simultaneous attention to dozens of details. One person who can do both is a blessing. Or find a director who can be the visionary and a supportive superintendent who keeps track of chalk, attendance forms, and people to recruit. Calling, training, and supporting good leadership are essential for a faithful program.

3. A full planning process culminating in a choice of curriculum is needed every few years.

The congregation needs to decide what it wants to accomplish. What will the child know at the end of a year in church school? What do adults need to wrestle with this next year? Everyone needs to participate in the planning process: parents, children, youth, adult learners, teachers, and pastor. It is the church's educational ministry, so the whole congregation needs to be invited into the process—the women's group, the men's breakfast group, the youth group. A daylong planning retreat where all interests come together may result in a mission statement so that it is possible to choose a curriculum. Once that is in place, the other questions are easy: when, where, who, how.

4. The management tasks of the staff and the committee responsible for the education program are endless.

But they come together in the following logic, in my view:

- A program for the whole church needs to include the children and to put them front and center. Jesus overturned tables and drove out money changers so that the children could be welcomed into the temple. We need to find every way to make them feel welcome in the chancel—receiving Bibles, participating in children's time, reading Scripture.
- The children will be adequately nurtured only if the adults are nurtured also. This aim may require a minimum two-and-a-half-hour commitment on Sunday morning: one hour for worship, one for learning, and a half hour for fellowship. Adult education needs to be carried out systematically.
- Spring is the busiest season for the Christian education program. All planning for the next fall needs to be done so that curricula can be ordered. All recruitment should be completed before families go on summer vacations. Most of us need to plan ahead before making a major time commitment. If no one was recruited last spring to teach, you have a problem, Lee. Those who have taught in the past will, one hopes, do it again since you are new. But that won't happen every year.
- The recruitment task is crucial. Frankly, I can't remember much of what was taught in the congregation in which I grew up. But I do remember the teachers. Most of them were terrific. You need to find those faithful, wonderful Christians. There are ways to do that well. If everyone understands that the teachers learn and grow as well as the students and that you provide them with a strong and excellent support system, recruiting teachers will be easier. People who have taught previously are your best choice to recruit teachers, rather than just one person, such as the pastor or the Christian education director. Someone who just finished teaching for three years and loved it can answer questions and persuade potential teachers to consider volunteering. One of the people I respect most in the field says she never accepts "no" as an answer. If someone can't teach, she suggests other opportunities, such as running a special program,

greeting new families, or serving on the committee. She finds some way for all to share in the educational mission of the church. Another educator says:

> The willingness to teach is not decided when you ask the question but long before—when it was decided to have a good curriculum, team teaching, reasonable terms of service, pleasant surroundings, ample supplies, people available to lend a hand at the last moment, and a church-wide commitment to Christian nurture.[1]

- Training teachers is an important support strategy. If people are to give up an evening or Saturday for training, that training program should be superb. As pastor, you need to be a part of it. Over time, include money in the budget to build a program, to bring educators in to teach your teachers, and to pay for teachers to attend events offered by the denomination or a seminary. Eventually, people will want to be teachers because it can help them learn how to be better parents as well.
- The genius is in the details—that is truer in the educational program than in any other. We need dreamers who have a vision of what might be ten years from now. But we also need people who can send a postcard to a sick child and someone who can find a substitute a half hour before class for the teacher who woke up with a migraine.

5. Don't forget special events.

The Advent workshop or Bible Sunday when children receive their first Bibles is important to the participants and lifts up the educational mission before the whole congregation. Invent new occasions. Host an open house when adults can visit the church school. Instead of the old-fashioned church-school Sunday, try a "Spring Fling" with a child-oriented meal (hot dogs instead of chicken) and a short program by the children for the adults. Or the adult class might lead the worship one Sunday.

6. A strong Christian education committee makes for a vital program.

Share in the leadership of that committee. While the core task of the committee is to establish policy, it should also be a hands-on working group that shares in both the adult and children's programs. It's hard to maintain balance between those two. But the quality of the program will depend largely on the quality of your education committee.

7. Finally, incorporate evaluation into your planning.

At the end of the year, find a way to ask students, teachers, and the congregation how they think the educational program has been going. Get into the habit of passing out evaluation forms after each event. You need feedback, but no one will offer it unless you invite them to do so.

I have not written these recommendations to overwhelm you, Lee. No church succeeds in doing everything every year. Help people do what can be done well, and agree to put off the rest for another time. Here, at the end of July, you are not going to do all I have suggested before the second weekend in September, unless others have already completed this work before you arrived. I hope this overview will help you make the choices that need to be made so that the best possible program can be put in place for this fall. Then feel good about it and thank God for what is possible.

Your fellow disciple,

Paul

CHAPTER 11

A System for Parish Care

August 12

Dear Lee,

Please don't apologize for writing so frequently. I know how much pressure you are under to get all these systems in place, and you must understand that I have more time in the summer than in the fall. Don't be embarrassed. I'll let you know if you write too often.

You are wondering about pastoral care. The search committee emphasized the need to do calling in the parish, and you'd like to address that need right off. Good for you! During the sixties, my first decade of ministry, a classmate I admire was outspoken and involved in the antiwar movement. Because I knew that many leaders in his congregation didn't share those sentiments, I asked how he got away with it. He said: "If you take care of the pastoral needs in the congregation, people will give you space to do anything else you want." I've remembered his point all these years, and he is right. If you are there for people, if you are present when times are difficult for parishioners, if you are professional and careful to serve the people's needs rather than your own ego—if you do all that with heart, feeling, and genuine affection, then you can be prophetic, controversial, even radical, and the most conservative congregation is still likely to affirm your leadership.

So how do you do it? Start with the principle, the theological base. There is a difference between pastoral care and parish care. Pastoral care is the ministry of the pastor, and I will talk about that later in this letter. But first let me speak of parish care—the caring community. The Reformation principle of the priesthood of all believers is its theological base. If you believe that you, as pastor, can take care of the congregation, you will end up believing you are indispensable, and the people you serve will see you as their savior. Instead, understand that your prime responsibility is to lead the community of caregivers. The first task is to create a system of care.

One Monday morning Brian came to my office to talk. He was only 56 years old and had been in sales his whole career. His company had just made him a generous offer for early retirement that he couldn't turn down. Now he wanted to know what he could do in the church as a volunteer. We both understood this situation to be a gift from God. As Brian put it, "What is it God would have me do these next years?" At the end of a week of conversations, his ministry was clear to both of us. For the next five years, Brian organized a system of parish care.

We started by exploring a national program that had just begun, the Stephen Ministry. This fine program is designed to do just what I am advocating: to build a system of recruiting, training, supporting, and celebrating lay ministry in congregations. That program is a real option for you, Lee, or at least a good model, even if you don't buy the package the organization is selling. A United Church of Christ notebook for lay caregivers, *Called to Care*, is worth considering, whatever one's denominational affiliation. It is more flexible and more economical than the Stephen Ministry.[1] Other organizations have viable programs to consider as well. This is how we proceeded with our program:

- We created a system with the congregation. We dreamed of a caring community in which we would all care for each other. Given that dream, we made clear who would do what. What care could only the pastor provide? What should be referred to professionals beyond the congregation? What could best be provided by lay members of the parish? Existing systems, such as the youth group, the women's group, and the men's breakfast group, joined in the effort. A large group of people divided the parish geographically with the understanding that every family would receive a personal visit or a phone call at least once a year. A smaller group of a dozen people agreed to visit the more needy families or individuals once a month.
- Training was provided for people in the whole system. The training varied for each group. The smaller group of a dozen people received the most intense training, but everyone in the congregation was

encouraged to attend one or two training sessions. Ultimately, the training benefits everyone. People want help in their own families with questions like: What are the resources in town available to us? How can I become a better listener? How do I deal with elderly parents? With dying friends? With a neighbor who talks about committing suicide?

• Finally, we tried to ground the whole effort in our mutual faith. We helped people learn how to pray aloud with others, we insisted that everyone keep a journal, and all training included theological reflection as a centerpiece.

It worked well while Brian was there to lead us. When he moved away, the program continued. The many people who had experienced the blessing of caring for another never stopped. But new people who followed Brian let the recruiting, training, and visibility fade, so that the program eventually disappeared from sight. The challenge is to find strong leaders who can keep the excitement alive.

I have tried to build a list of things I watch for. After one of our dearest members died in a fire in her home, I urged every visitor to check discreetly for smoke alarms. Make a mental note of whether the house is clean. I don't mean we ought to pick at people who are not "neatniks," but if an elderly person is living in a filthy room, we have a responsibility to match that person up with a good cleaning service, and to help pay for it if that is necessary. Above all, watch for signs of neglect or abuse. If you come across a household with six young children and a kitchen sink full of the same clothes waiting to be hand-washed two weeks running, it's likely that no one is cooking in the house. If an elderly man rolls his eyes and shakes his fist at you, he may be signaling that his caretaker in the next room is abusive. If a woman has a black eye, pay attention.

In fact, I have tried to become an expert on abuse. It's a real problem in most of our congregations. Know who has keys to the church building so that an abuser doesn't use it as a place to injure a child. Run background checks on workers with youth and children to make certain that they are not likely to put those young people at risk. Premarital counseling has revealed shocking information on more than one occasion. One young woman told me that she had been abused as a child by her father and wondered what impact that would have on her marriage. A bride-to-be came into my study for the first premarital counseling session and said, with tears in her eyes, "The last time I was in this office, I was 13 and the minister at that time made a pass at me."

One of the most important questions I ask myself as I go from house to house, from nursing home to hospital bed, is: "What is real here?" Is this a happy home or is it abusive? Is there a real reason for all the guilt this person is expressing, or is it a sign of something else? Are there legitimate reasons for this woman to be so fearful, or has she been watching too many television news programs and talk shows?

An awareness of the holy is the most significant thing I bring to a visit. People who are living on the edge, those who are in real pain, the elderly who are alone—these people spend much time thinking about God. Some of their thoughts are irrational, like the notion that God is punishing them for some childhood sin. But more often, their musing is on the mark, like that of the elderly woman who told me, "Living alone brings you closer to God—you have time to be aware, to listen, to really pray." People yearn for the ear of someone from the church community who will be honest in speaking about God. They will not always agree with your definition of reality, but they will appreciate the opportunity to talk about it.

I have been talking about parish care, the caring community of the whole church, and your leadership role. Let's move on to pastoral care —the care that only the pastor can give. You bring something special as an ordained minister, Lee, and more than just the sacrament of Holy Communion. Church folk feel that the pastor embodies a special aura, a unique gift. How do you find the time, energy, and wisdom to share that gift?

It's hard to visit people in modern communities in this country. Few people are home in the afternoon; and evenings are filled with night classes, school events, and other meetings. Weekends are a zoo of activity in most families. When do you visit? Some important events will serve as triggers for you to be present, and on these occasions people will make time for your visit.

- Illness is an obvious occasion to be with a church member. That can be hard—hospital stays are increasingly brief these days; often people are in hospitals a good distance from home. But the real problem is inside us: We don't like to be with people who are really sick. To spend time with a friend who is dying, a child who is profoundly ill, a young mother who has just learned that the cancer has returned—

none of that is easy. People say, "How can you stand being with
people in trouble all the time?" The truth is that it is not depressing;
the courage, the ability to cope, the strength of dying people is mi-
raculous. Being in their presence is a privilege.

- Grief is another obvious need that demands attention. When a death
  occurs, many people still want the pastor to be called before the
  mortician. We have talked about what to do to prepare for a funeral.
  But the important time is after the memorial service, after the family
  has gone, after the world assumes everything is fine. You need to
  be there on the anniversary of the death—the first week, the first
  Christmas, Easter, or birthday. When you hear of the murder of a
  teenage boy on the evening news, look in on the parents whose
  teenager was killed five years ago. They probably saw the program
  too, and the news report brought it all back. You are an expert on
  grief in a culture that hates and ignores the grieving process. It must
  be a priority for you.
- Dozens of circumstances mark a change in a person's life. Each is
  an opportunity for you to be present. A wedding is a real change in
  the lives of the couple's parents; a baptism is a great time to help
  parents establish a family dynamic that has integrity for them. A
  child goes off to college; a member gets laid off from work; a deacon is the guilty party in a public scandal. All of those moments are
  occasions for pastoral ministry.

You have studied this subject in seminary, Lee. I can't add much to
that except these few practical habits that I have found helpful. I try to
take the initiative and not wait to be asked to visit or inquire. God took
the initiative with us; we need to be bold with others. The whole world
is reactive—"If they want help, let them ask." That is not the pastoral
ministry. Don't be afraid of what you will say or see or feel. You can
trust both yourself and the Holy Spirit; most people want your help.
Trust your own intuition. If you feel uncomfortable or uneasy, don't
ignore that feeling. There are situations in which you need to be careful
for your personal or professional safety. I keep a record of those visits
and conversations—nothing formal or public, but enough for my defense
in court or before an ecclesiastical council should the need arise. At the
same time, I am not one to keep records of counseling sessions. If there
is nothing written down, I feel safer keeping the confidence. I do keep
notes on what we have done in premarital counseling, what I want to

remember after the funeral—names, useful images, poignant comments. I also believe we benefit from reflecting on how we felt after a significant visit or meeting.

Finally, one of the most helpful tools in parish care is the small group. When public school teachers were discouraged after working with no contract for three years, we gathered them together for mutual support in the context of the faith community. When the economy soured and several people were laid off, when nurses felt unappreciated, when several parents of teenagers were overwhelmed, when a group of people in the church who opposed my leadership talked about me in the parking lot—in each case, we gathered people into a small support group. The leadership of these groups must be relevant to the situation as well as to the faith context. I have always loved these groups, even the ones that don't like my leadership.

You can see from this letter that parish care requires a wonderful memory for the details of the lives of a lot of people. The computer is a blessing. Even the smallest church can usually afford a computer and database software. Into that database you can program all sorts of pastoral detail while honoring confidentiality, and every week the computer will remind you who needs attention.

In closing, remember that, as pastor, you are nurtured as you care for the congregation. That happens in two ways. First, whenever I feel depressed at work, when it seems that I'm wasting my life, I visit people in the congregation. It's not just that they build up my ego (although it is true that being needed helps in that regard), but rather that parish care gets me out of the office and in touch with the people God has called into Christ's church. Second, when someone in our family is in need, the parish-care system serves us as well. When I had back surgery, I realized how wonderful that care was. When my colleague had breast cancer, the ministry she received from her congregation overwhelmed her.

Thank God for the church that nurtures us all.

Your grateful colleague,

Paul

CHAPTER 12

Stewardship That Works

August 20

Dear Lee,

I knew you'd be asking about fund-raising here at the end of the summer. You describe the giving as very low at Central Church; your stewardship drive consists of a photocopied letter put together at the last minute by the pastor and committee chair and sent by third-class mail to all households. That is really sad, but you need to know that most congregations in mainline denominations are stuck in exactly that pattern. Leadership is required from all of us who care about the future of the church. So this is an important subject—a theological subject.

Every community, be it a congregation or a city or a nation, has a culture—a way of believing and behaving that has been learned and shared in such a way that the community can survive generation after generation. Every congregation has a culture of giving, a pattern that has been used over the decades. Culture is not easily changed. People make values of the patterns that have evolved and with which they lived over the years. I will discuss with you some other time the apostle Paul's belief in "principalities and powers"—what biblical theologian Walter Wink calls "the church's angel." We mistakenly think that when the old guard dies or moves away, things will change. But that doesn't happen because new members are acculturated into the old system. We believe that Christ has power to overcome principalities, powers, angels, and cultures. That is the stewardship task at Central Church, Lee: to expose the culture of giving to Jesus Christ in such a way that it, along with all of us, can be transformed.

Let me be specific about the culture of giving and the ways it needs to be changed. Then I will talk about strategies for change. Finally I will make some suggestions about what you might do between now and your fund-raising Sunday.

The culture of giving in this country's mainline Protestant churches can be described according to eight patterns or assumptions. Here's what needs to happen in each case to make them effective and faithful.

1. *The pyramid of generosity.* Twenty percent of the people give 80 percent of the total pledge. That means that a few families support most of the church's budget every year. Everyone knows about this pyramid. The top two or three givers in the church know they are at the top, and everyone else knows too. The smallest givers know they are at the bottom of the pyramid, along with the largest number of people, and they don't care because they are inactive. This dollar-a-week pledge is about all they do in the church. If they are to increase their annual gift, they will have to deepen their faith commitments. The culture says nothing can be done about the pyramid. The top givers, who believe they are doing more than their share, form a ceiling that defines the whole pyramid; their refusal to increase their gift influences those at the bottom, who see no reason to give more than $52 a year. Two things need to happen here: first, the whole pyramid needs to move up so that the lowest and highest gift are not the same as they were in 1942. Second, the inactive people on the bottom of the pyramid need to become more involved in the faith community.

2. *Democratic giving as a value.* This assumption questions the existence of a pyramid: "If all 100 of us gave one-hundredth of the budget, we would all be happy." Those in the top half of the pyramid tend to make that argument. In its simplicity it is totally wrong, for some people can't afford to give one-hundredth of the total budget of the church. What we need is proportional giving—that is, each of us giving a portion of what we have received: ten percent, five percent, one percent of our income—let each decide. Proportional giving recognizes the generosity of the widow's mite. In other words, people who have little and give a large percentage of what they have are actually contributing more than those who are rich but whose large donation is a tiny fraction of their real wealth. Again, we need to hold people to the truth of proportional giving by explaining the theology and the economy of church life again and again.

3. *The rule of secrecy.* Privacy is a value in mainline churches. This notion assumes that what I give is between God and me. No one on the stewardship committee should know; the pastor should be kept in the dark, lest he or she give more pastoral attention to those who give more or embarrass me publicly because of my small gift. People shouldn't reveal their own pledges, for that might make other people feel uncomfortable if they have less to give. The rule of secrecy maintains the current culture of giving. If no one can talk openly about his or her own giving, others will not be challenged to change their patterns of giving. This secrecy assures all that they will not be challenged to give more, since it presumes their generosity as fact. I am not suggesting that we post members' names and the amount of each one's gift on the bulletin board. But I do think that the stewardship committee needs to know so that families can be visited by someone who gives in their approximate range. I think the pastor can be trusted with this information; it can also help the pastor understand the spirituality of each family. I think everyone needs to understand where he or she stands on the pyramid in relation to everyone else and thereby be challenged to move up a step.

4. *Holding back something for the special appeals.* Most mainline churches ask people to pledge for the year and give by the week. This system allows the congregation's leadership to write an annual budget, and it allows giving to be part of the liturgy. But denominations periodically plan special offerings. Financial emergencies in the parish also prompt special appeals. Having become used to this pattern, people hold back from their annual pledge something for those situations. In fact, many hold back far more than they will ever contribute in a given year to all special offerings imaginable. I think we need to cut back on special offerings, announce them ahead of time, and teach people that the church will live on the income in the budget and not depend on special appeals.

5. *False assumptions.* People make two assumptions to justify a small gift. First, some assume that the congregation is rolling in money and doesn't need a large donation. This conversation occurs in the parking lot or the grocery store: "Consider all the special funds the church has:

memorial funds, invested funds, emergency funds. There always seems to be enough money for the pastor's favorite project. They don't really need my money. After all, I don't have any special funds anywhere." Second, other people assume that the church is broke and isn't going to make it through the decade: "Giving generously to that outfit is funding a lost cause." This assumption is spoken not in the parking lot or the grocery store, but in the boardroom or golf club by those at the very top of the pyramid: "If I give all that I can afford to give, the church will be dependent on my generosity." Of course, each assumption holds a shred of truth. The trouble is, people make both assumptions to justify a stingy gift. The church needs to educate people about the financial realities of church life and thus help them connect their giving and their faith. Every time a major bequest is made to the endowment, we need to celebrate it and explain the importance of the endowment. Every time a room is painted, we need to identify the source of the money to fund the project. Every deficit needs to be followed by an explanation of how church leadership plans to address it.

6. *Avoidance of "pushiness."* Most congregations assume that they shouldn't ask people to give more than they are prepared to give. "Just lay out the need, explain the budget, and people will be generous." That is either naïve (people are intrinsically generous) or self-serving (don't ask me to give more than I am used to giving). Now I am not suggesting that we name a price for membership in the church. But let's be honest about what we hope people will consider giving.

7. *The relationship of commitment to contribution.* We assume that people "get faith" and then give. But how do we encourage those at the bottom of the pyramid to increase their gifts? Common wisdom suggests getting people involved in the church program and then asking for money. Perhaps we miss Jesus' point in saying, "Where your treasure is, there your heart will be also." If you ask the top givers, many will say they first gave generously and then got involved. Many people like fund-raising and are good at it. They offer to serve the church in that way and fall in love with the Gospel in the process!

8. *Giving for services rendered.* The assumption is that when my needs are met, I will give. Consumerism is alive and well in the faith community. First produce what I want; then I will pay. This is no exaggeration.

We all know people who cut back on their contribution to the church because the church hasn't done anything for them in over a year. That means these people aren't giving at all; rather, they are buying a service. Faith becomes a commodity for sale. If I don't need it this year, then I'll not pay this year. The very idea of giving is absent in the consumer mindset. The theology that claims God's gift has already been granted, and that our giving is simply a response to that unspeakably wonderful grace of Jesus Christ, is totally absent in the consumer's consciousness. We urgently need a conversion from being consumers who pay for services rendered to being Christians who give to others because God gave everything to us.

There are other ways of describing the culture of giving. The question is, What strategies will help liberate us from the constraints of the culture in most of our churches?

One strategy is the *capital-fund drive*; some say that congregations need to conduct one every ten years. I was shocked when I first heard that statement, but now I believe it. A major capital fund effort stretches people. A professional consultant can teach lay leaders how to run a good fund-raising effort. A well-run capital drive will raise the tide of annual giving to the church. This effect is not magic. Hard work changes the culture by (1) addressing the top givers separately and forcefully, (2) asking people for a contribution that falls within a specific dollar range, and (3) resulting in a tangible difference in the life of the church that everyone can see and in which all can take pride. The capital-fund drive moves the whole pyramid up.

A second strategy is the *annual fund drive*. You have probably noticed the problem I have in naming this annual event. Many traditions refer to it as the "stewardship drive." In some respects, that's a great way to describe it: we are all stewards of God's world and need to care for it by using the talents God has given us. The trouble is that stewardship is about more than money—it describes the whole of the Christian life. This name also defers to those who don't want to talk about money in the church. I'd rather give it a more honest and direct name: the fund-raising drive. But the name is perhaps the last thing about the culture of giving we need to change.

I favor a three-year cycle in planning annual fund drives. This span provides a range of options. Doing the same thing two years in a row can

result in a loss of effectiveness. Let me list some options. The first requires the most work to run, but the results are the most satisfying. At
the bottom is the easiest way to raise money, but it challenges few people
to increase their giving. What works best is a range of efforts that differ
year by year.

1. Visit every family in the parish—member and nonmember, elderly
    retiree and college student. On the one hand, this is a time to talk
    about life in the church, to learn what people find satisfying and
    frustrating. But the deeper purpose is to talk about giving, what we
    give and what we hope others will give. That might be a dollar
    amount; it might be a step up the published pyramid. Visitation-
    team members need to be carefully trained and should not be asked
    to visit more than five households. It's a huge task, but it works best
    of all.

2. Invite the congregation to small-group meetings in homes of mem-
    bers. Ask the host to provide a meal or dessert, and recruit another
    person to moderate the discussion. Focus the participation on what
    people love about the church, what would strengthen it, and some
    straight talk about money. Again, request a specific response that
    will stretch people's giving patterns. This approach also requires
    much work. Descriptions of the church's life, its financial needs,
    and top-quality leadership in each group are key. Most important,
    the makeup of each group should reflect the spectrum of opinion in
    the congregation.

3. Telephone each member of the congregation on a given day. Tell
    everyone about the plan, and prepare a different script for each type
    of giver and nongiver. Train the callers carefully so that they don't
    go through the motions to collect a "same as last year" pledge card.
    A frank and honest conversation about the church and about giving
    is possible on the phone. If there are several phone extensions in a
    home, several family members can participate. These calls are hard
    work. It helps to install a bank of phones so that all the callers can
    be in the same room with some refreshments and mutual support.

4. Mail out a copy of the budget and a pledge card to each member.
    Carefully word the letter and the supporting materials to make the

needs clear. One way to improve on the mass mailing is to write different letters to top givers, fringe members, new members, youth, and nongivers. If feasible, address the letters by hand and send them by first-class mail. Many people don't open bulk mail.

There are infinite variations among these four. A couple of methods I would try last. One is "Pony Express," which has been popular in recent years. Members carry a mail sack, filled with pledge cards and sealable envelopes, from door to door. No one speaks to anyone about anything, except a greeting at the door as the visitor deposits the pouch. The recipient delivers it to the next household on the route. It's a great way to save on postage but a poor way to raise money for anything as important as the church of Jesus Christ. Even below that, I believe, would rank the "Faith Promise" program. Those who attend worship on the designated Sunday hear a rousing sermon, and then write an amount on a "faith promise" card—but no name. The leadership has a figure to use to build a budget, and no one knows what anyone else has promised. The church leadership's "leap of faith" in the people is meant to inspire generosity. And, for better or worse, it maintains secrecy.

You will understand that the success of the annual drive depends on the committee in charge. You can either educate your nominating committee to find the best candidates or manipulate the nominating process to get your candidates elected. The worst situation is to end up with committee members who are among the lowest givers in the church and who have a vested interest in maintaining that meager status. The best committee represents the wide spectrum of giving patterns in the parish.

A third strategy, *planned giving*, affords people the opportunity to give in such a way that they can use the money for the rest of their lives, with the understanding that when they die, it will belong to the designated beneficiary. It is a scandal that congregations do not help members with planned giving. The tax savings to the donor and the financial benefit to the charitable organization are both substantial. People need to understand that their beloved congregation, judicatory, or mission agency can benefit if included in a donor's will. Making a conditional gift provides a large tax benefit to the donor. Hospitals, colleges, and social-service agencies all routinely arrange for such gifts from their constituencies, which include church members.

Why are we so reluctant to introduce this alternative to our members? First, it takes time to understand the systems and to educate the congregation. Second, the benefit is delayed, and congregations are shortsighted enough to believe that their priority is to raise money for this year's budget. But the biggest deterrents are the church's ambivalence and ignorance about endowment funds. Back in the fifties it was popular to believe that the healthy church lived from year to year on people's current contributions. But economic realities made that hand-to-mouth theology nothing short of madness in the seventies. Most church structures were overbuilt in the fifties by people who believed the growth would last forever. Twenty years later a congregation of 150 families found itself supporting a building erected when the membership was twice that size. When John D. Rockefeller paid to build Riverside Church in Manhattan, he also contributed an endowment to pay for its upkeep. Nearly every congregation needs to raise an endowment for its church and for the church of its children's generation. We know that endowments are required for a seminary, a college, a hospital. Why should the congregation be an exception to that economic reality? Planned gifts and bequests are necessary if the body of Christ is to survive in the real world.

The congregation has to have a sensible investment policy if it is to benefit from planned giving or bequests. People are not going to turn large bequests over to a church if they suspect that the congregation will squabble over how the money is to be invested or used. A clear investment policy is not easy to write. For example, some in the congregation will want the policy to be socially responsible, excluding investments in companies whose business practices or products they consider unacceptable. Some will want the portfolio invested for growth, while others will want more security. Some will want to specify how the income is to be used, while others will trust the church to decide how to use the income each year and in each budget. I believe the congregation needs to vote on the investment policy. Much work will have to be done over a significant time period. Only if you deal with these issues now will peo-ple know that Central Church is able to use their bequest responsibly.

In this letter I have tried to share some of the issues and strategies that need to be included in a congregation's institutional life. I am aware that your initial question focused on this fall's fund drive, which begins November 1. Your first task is to form a strong committee to plan for the long run. Communication is the only way any institution can raise money. If people know the church has a plan to raise money, and if they know what that plan is, they will give.

November 1 is not a big problem. This is your honeymoon, after all. Everyone loves you and wants you to succeed. This is the year everyone is motivated to contribute to the church's bright future. All you have to do is to get the church leadership to tell people the truth about what is needed, ask them for a specific gift to address that need, and work hard between now and the end of October to make it happen.

With the help of the nominating committee, choose a strong committee or, if you inherit a weak one, augment it with strong people to act as consultants. You need not only people who are strong givers but also members of diverse gifts—some who can think about the big picture and others who can remember the small details.

Decide by the end of September on the shape of the annual drive. Don't try to conduct an every-member visitation this year. You don't have time for that. But don't send out the same old mailing either. Pick something new, some process that is possible to accomplish in this short time frame.

Get lots of people involved—organizing, making phone calls, cooking meals, writing letters. And plan carefully to follow through. After November 1 you need a plan to get all the late pledges in and a final celebration at the worship service on Thanksgiving Sunday. But even now, start a few of those people thinking about what the church will do to raise money in the next three years.

Finally, there is the matter of your personal example, Lee. The truth is that no one's pledge is a total secret, especially not the pastor's. You need to be in the upper portion of the giving pyramid, even though your salary is not. Your witness along with the witness of the whole committee is key.

Christ gave everything, even life itself, for us. Given that grace, we can at least consider a tithe.

Yours in the name of that gracious Christ Jesus,

Paul

CHAPTER 13

Education for Mission

September 22

Dear Lee,

When you accepted a call to serve a New England congregation, you understood that September would be the wildest month in your year. In New England, people tend to stay away from church in the summer months. That means everything must be up and running immediately after everyone has been away for the previous nine weeks. But you survived it and, from your description, it went well. Congratulations! It sounds as if the honeymoon is still on. Make it last as long as you can.

You asked for my thoughts on the request you received to hold a monthly food collection in the narthex every communion Sunday. You are a little hesitant because you know nothing about the food pantry that will benefit, the proposed program doesn't offer your members an opportunity to meet the food recipients, and no one seems to be asking what the congregation might do to help these people get back on their feet. That is a great set of questions.

First, let's talk about the mission committee that would administer the program. You say the committee meets regularly but limits its work to the question of how to spend the mission budget. What do you think the committee ought to do? I think a better strategy is to focus its energies on educating the congregation for mission. A subcommittee can make proposals for budget allocation. If committee members undertake that larger teaching task, their efforts will translate into more money to spend on mission each year.

All year long, the church's mission must be made visible to the congregation. Explain how mission money goes from the local church to support the work of the denomination and the mission beyond our church. If we ask people to give in proportion to their income, then the church also needs to give a percentage of its total budget to mission, and even the mission committee should give a percentage (I suggest two-thirds) of the total mission budget to denominational mission. Show how some of the mission budget supports local agencies that work in rural areas, in small towns, in seminaries, and in cities. A description of the relevant church polity may sound dull, but it can be spruced up with a brisk multimedia presentation. All of that needs to be explained a dozen times a year—to new members, to new committee members, to church organizations as the budget is being built, and when the money is being raised. This presentation needs to dance!

But that brief road show won't do the trick alone, no matter how good it is. The truth is that most congregations and pastors don't believe in "mission." They see it as paternalistic cultural imperialism. The problem is that most of us here at the turn of the millennium have a 19th-century understanding of mission. Begin with an education program to introduce people to today's theology of mission. A number of helpful resources are available, including a small book for laypeople that I wrote, *Mission: A Parish Perspective.*[1]

We need to be innovative if people are to catch on to what God's mission is in our church. For example:

- Establish a relationship with a church in Asia, Africa, or Latin America.
- Welcome a missionary for a weekend.
- Missionaries go both ways. See if you can arrange for a missionary from another land to work with your congregation for a time.
- Encourage members to visit the mission when they travel.
- Encourage denominational nominating committees to name your church members to national mission boards.
- Be a pest. People should say, "There she goes, thumping the tub for mission again." The pastor should say, "If I don't promote the global mission on World Communion Sunday, that mission committee will have my neck."

Part of education is promotion. When the church budget is being written, when the every-member visitation teams are trained, when the men's group is planning the year's program, when the finance committee is trimming expenses to match income, when the Christian education committee is planning the curriculum—on all those occasions the mission committee representative needs to be present.

A myth in congregations holds that the finance committee and the mission committee are competitors. To the contrary, mission drives the whole budget. Money given to nurture children in the faith is mission money, as are the budgets for worship, pastoral salaries, and building upkeep. Make a list of the groups in town that use the church building at little or no cost. That's mission too. When church leaders come to see that the whole budget is mission, they don't decide to give less to the mission committee and keep more in the local expense budget. They recognize that people would rather give to God's work in the world than to the fuel or maintenance budget. People will in fact give more to both local mission and mission to others. It is no longer a question of how large a slice each is going to get. The pie itself will be larger because people will give more.

Education for mission will build, year after year. I suggest this goal: within five years, no one should dare raise money to put a new roof on your church without also planning to contribute to a new roof for a mission the church supports.

Seen in this light, the suggestion to become a partner with the food pantry is a gift. It gives the congregation an opportunity to move education for mission from theory to practice. I suggest you start where the people are, and with enthusiasm. Food for the hungry! Let everyone feel good about it. Then structure some opportunities to reflect on the project, and encourage church members to ask the questions you have asked. Help them understand that if it's really mission, it needs to be done in partnership with the people who are hungry. Some will volunteer to serve the food, sit down and eat it with the recipients, and get to know them. You can encourage those volunteers to share their experience with others. Gradually they will come to ask why these people are in need— is it mental illness, an addiction, a series of bad breaks? They will then begin to ask how they can help these people out of poverty and prevent others from slipping into life on the streets. Imagine more and more people sharing this ministry at the food pantry. Eventually all will begin to ask, What is the church? Who is in and who is out? What is the difference between the church and the country club? Where does Jesus Christ fit into all of this?

This project seems exciting when I describe it that way. But it is frightening also. Inevitably, some of these homeless people from the food pantry are going to come to worship— just to see what it's all about. Not everyone will be happy to see them. Those who want a safer, more comfortable religion will stand over against those who welcome vulnerability and openness. The conflict will start with questions of taste, dress, and hygiene. But, I warn you, it is just a matter of time before the questions become far more dangerous. "Why are we allowing these strangers who are so different from ourselves into our sanctuary? Think about our safety, our children, our image as a congregation." The tension is part of the gift.

If you are faithful in your leadership, people will gradually see the connection between these new visitors and the woman at the well. Remember her? At noon, in the heat of the day when no one else was at the well, she came to draw water. Her reputation was so sordid that she dared not go to the well when other women were there. She was not only a foreigner, she was a fallen woman. Jesus stopped, asked her for a drink, and talked with her. We come to understand the meaning of that encounter only when our prejudice is exposed, when we are asked to stop and talk with someone we had always assumed was evil. In that moment, when we recognize our own bias, we are free of the burden of prejudice. You need to understand the peril. Some will probably turn on you, just as they turned on Jesus. But that too is an opportunity to witness to the power of the cross.

I am not suggesting a posture of martyrdom. You will find a way to lead the congregation through the conflict to a resolution that allows most members to rejoice in the outcome, because they will see that the church is more than a dressed-up ritual for the middle class.

Many experts claim that vital congregations excel in three areas of the church's life: innovative worship, high-quality Christian education, and an excellent mission program. The point of this letter, then, is to encourage you not only to educate for mission but also to welcome every opportunity to bring the mission of God home to your people.

Your partner in mission,

Paul

CHAPTER 14

The Church Crisis

October 8

Dear Lee,

Less than four months after your arrival in the parish, the fear of conflict
has become real. That is not unusual, Lee. Let me see if I understand the
situation. Three members of the congregation, all of whom served on the
search committee that called you and whom you respect, told you of
their conviction that yours ought to be an "Open and Affirming Congregation"—a congregation that welcomes and affirms gays and lesbians.
They talked with you because you are new; if you ask, they will delay
initiating this movement until you are more settled and know the congregation better. You know from other congregations (as well as from
President Clinton's experience with this issue in the first months of his
first term) that this will be a divisive matter. Your question is this: Would
it be wise to wait until you are "in the saddle," or is this the way you
establish yourself as leader?

Where two or three are gathered together, there is conflict. Consider Paul's letters to the early churches: Almost all of those letters deal
with conflict. The gospels are no different; Jesus was a controversial
figure. The history of the church is the story of turmoil, division, and
warfare within the church. People in congregations that are profoundly
divided sing about "the fellowship of kindred minds" without noting the
irony. When I began seminary, I thought that the pastor was the most
beloved person in town, at least from what I knew of my hometown pastor. I soon learned that that pastor was both loved and despised. When I
arrived in my first parish in the 1960s, it was clear that this vocation

would not satisfy my appetite for popularity. Conflict has been a constant companion. In this letter I hope to convince you that conflict isn't necessarily a bad companion; indeed, it can be a good friend.

Why is that? Conflict and commitment go together. If we really don't care what the church is, we won't fight for what we want it to be. But people care so passionately about their faith that they are ready to fight until they win and quit if they lose. Because they care so deeply, these faithful people don't just quietly walk out of the church when they disagree with it; rather, they stomp out with a dramatic flair and invite others to join them.

The "Open and Affirming" issue is a lightning rod that will surely ignite that kind of passionate controversy. We are talking about core issues here: the definition of masculinity, what it means to be a woman. We are talking about homosexuality in the church where your mom and dad never heard the word *sex* mentioned, much less in an "open and affirming" way! Our sexuality and our spirituality are linked in a potent tension. This conflict is dynamite; it could explode.

Look at the issue from the pastor's point of view. The wonderful thing about being a pastor is that we meet people where life really matters to them, not just for small talk. The issues presented to us are of great consequence: marriage, parenthood, and career—all of these are conflicted precisely *because* they matter. Our business is conflict—in the lives of people and in the life of the community. If we shy away from conflict, we shy away from the pastoral ministry itself. People are watching you in these first months. They want to know if you can be trusted with their troubles. They have you on trial: "Can Lee be trusted?" How you choose to handle this "Open and Affirming" initiative will be a crucial piece of evidence in this all-important proceeding. You dare not shrink from conflict; yet if you embrace it, many will judge you harshly.

A friend of mine is a church consultant who helps congregations, in his words, to "move from conflict to community." It's an important ministry; consultants can be handy when life gets hard. Although conflict is a healthy sign that people care, it can easily turn so bitter that church members and pastors are forced to leave. Dayl Hufford of Andover Newton Theological School observes that when people face change, it often produces conflict. We have been taught from childhood not to show our anger, not to be afraid, not to cry in public. If we can't express our anger, fear, or sadness, if we keep it all inside, we will be conflicted.

Sometimes you will need to move from conflict to community; to do so you may need the help of someone from outside the congregation. I want to talk with you about the conflict that exists before it is identified as a problem. In fact, that is where you are now. No one knows of a problem to be solved, no sides have been taken. But now is the time to prevent "fighting or fleeing"; now is the time to prevent church members from getting hurt. The way you behave now, the example you set, the witness you make can prevent terrible trouble from breaking out later on.

The conflict I am talking about is the creative and inevitable sort that offers a wonderful opportunity to grow. This kind of conflict isn't what you escape to find community; this conflict *is* community where people of different perspectives live together in a single church. As pastor of this community, you know how different the people are, how angry the members would be if they knew how others felt. You lie awake at night praying, "God, how can I hold this congregation together another month?" There is no escaping this kind of conflict. But pastors learn some leadership strategies that help. Here's my list.

1. *Remember that the pastor is called to serve the whole congregation.* When a small group of people in a congregation I served proposed that we become a "sanctuary church" by accepting illegal aliens from Nicaragua to embarrass the Reagan administration, we had conflict. Since most of the members had voted for President Reagan, the outcome was predictable. The conflict began with a wonderful education process about important questions: What is the situation in Latin America? What is American foreign policy? What is the role of the church? Is it ethical to break the law and welcome an illegal alien? Then the opponents organized and held a series of events from their perspective. I provided administrative support to both sides. That support was often misunderstood to mean that I agreed with one side or the other. That might be a problem, but it's not as bad as if one side had the support of the church office for mailings and the other did not. That would not be fair. You are pastor to those who want to begin the process toward becoming an "Open and Affirming" body, as well as to those who oppose that action. If power is exercised unfairly, the conflict will deepen.

2. *Be honest.* Sitting on the fence is not a helpful posture. It is far better
to go public with your position and also with your commitment to respect and be the pastor of those who do not agree with you. In the sixties
I said, "I am going to Washington, D.C., to march with Dr. King, but if
you disagree with my position on civil rights, that doesn't mean you
should leave this congregation." Most people respected that position. If
you believe the church should be an Open and Affirming community, as
I gather you do, you need to be clear about where you stand. Being two-
faced is a strategy for disaster. In the sanctuary-movement issue I was in
the embarrassing position of not being clear where I stood. On the one
hand, I believed in opposing U.S. foreign policy toward Nicaragua and
thought that the sanctuary movement was a clever way to expose the
folly of that policy. On the other hand, I knew that many church members would feel obliged to leave the congregation if the church took a
stand that was illegal. I was not sure that church membership should
require allegiance to a political point of view. I was honestly on the
fence and was severely criticized by both sides. Even in that circum-
stance, honesty is best.

3. *Get all the information from all sides out in the open.* One cause of
lethal conflict is the lack of accurate information. When people don't
know the facts of a situation, they supply their own "facts" based on
assumptions, usually false. One church I served had an ongoing battle
between the weekday nursery school and the church. The congregation's
financial reports were not clear. Did the nursery school underwrite the
church budget, or did the church financially support the school? Everyone supplied his or her own interpretation to support an individual bias.
Get the facts out early and often.

4. *Recognize that most conflicts are not simple.* It takes time for
church leaders to clarify the facts and more time for the membership to
believe what the leadership says. If we rush toward resolution before we
agree on the facts, the conflict will worsen. This issue you're considering, Lee, of welcoming gays and lesbians into the church and into the
ordained ministry, must not be rushed. Take as much time as you need
to consider it. The time will not be wasted. In that interval people can
come to a deeper understanding of what homosexuality is and what the
church is.

5. *Work toward a win/win solution.* If one side wins and the other loses, it usually means that, in fact, both sides lose. The sanctuary issue turned into a victory for both sides. The question came before the church's annual meeting. The sanctuary opponents called all church members, explained the anti-sanctuary viewpoint, and urged them to attend. A mob turned out—five to one against becoming a sanctuary church. Some opponents were mean-spirited, accusing the supporters of being communists, unchristian, and wicked. The hate was heaped specifically on the man who had organized the move for sanctuary. The verbal attack was as close to a crucifixion as I had ever witnessed. The object of hate was truly Christlike in his grace. He did not shout back or retaliate. I believe it was because of that man's gracious spirit that the whole crowd, that very night, agreed that although we should not become a sanctuary church, we should strive to establish a partnership with a church in Latin America. That partnership continues to this day. Keep looking for the win/win possibilities.

6. *Lose gracefully.* The leader of the pro-sanctuary group showed uncommon grace in defeat, and that led the way to a resolution. When we first arrived at that parish, a group of educators, including Jackie, worked hard on a proposal for a day-care center in an unused wing of the church building. It is a complicated task to write such a proposal that complies with a knee-deep stack of state regulations. When it came to the church council, the proposal was voted down. Some told others that I would find a way to get the proposal passed, especially since my wife had worked so hard on it. I was clear that the council had spoken, and that was the end of it. I believe that was an important step in the task of building trust. We expect church members to lose gracefully; pastors must be ready to do the same.

7. *Know that forgiveness isn't easy.* This point came clear for me in working with abused women, who often believe that to forgive the abuser simply frees him to abuse again. The road to forgiveness is long. Most congregations are full of old grudges. Long ago a conflict erupted over worship style. It was settled with a compromise acceptable to most, but the opposing sides never dealt with their feelings toward one another. Each subsequent conflict found the same people lined up against each other. In time everyone knew who was angry with whom, but no one could remember why. Forgiveness is the prize that comes at the end of the reconciliation. It is the goal toward which we must work. The central point of the Christian faith is that God has forgiven us; therefore we are free to break the circle of blame and rage by forgiving others. But it is not helpful to ask the wronged party in a conflict to forgive before we have helped that person down the road of reconciliation that includes both repentance and grace.

8. *Establish an appropriate emotional tone.* You are the one who sets the tone. If you are frightened, defensive, skittish, hesitant, or anxious about this "Open and Affirming" issue, people will know. Every congregation is an expert at reading the pastor's mood. Many pastors have unintentionally escalated an issue from a small spat to a huge, divisive battle by their own high anxiety level.

9. *Maintain trust.* This last point is most important of all. First, trust the congregation. I sense in you a worry about the importance of being both open *and* affirming. If the resolution were to lose or if the vote were to be "open but not affirming," closeted gay or lesbian members might be offended and feel forced to find another church community. In that case, you would want to go with them. You can't say that to anyone, for it would sound like a threat: If you don't vote my way, I'll quit. But it isn't fair to introduce the process if you can't be honest about what is at stake. Trust the congregation you serve. The members were smart enough to call you and entrust the congregation to your care; you need to trust them in return. Remember, the proposal is not to decide whether to become an Open and Affirming Congregation, but rather to begin the exploration into that proposition. Step by step, the process will move ahead. Most congregations take two years to reach a resolution. Trust the church to be diligent, careful, and sensitive in its exploration. Beginning the process does not mean that the church can't stop in the middle if it is clear that no resolution is possible.

Second, trust yourself. Is this a lethal conflict in which you are being set up, or is it a faithful outreach to meet a real need? Is the church ready to begin the first steps along this path, or would it be better to wait until you have spent a little more time as its pastor? Trust your feelings. Take time to explore your heart. What lies behind your hesitance? Why are you so eager to march forward? You are a healthy, well-balanced human being. When you are clear about who you are and how you feel, go with that instinct.

Finally, in the real world of the church, the wonderful and frightening truth is that the pastor can't control the agenda. The Holy Spirit has a way of blocking us from one intended path and leading us toward others we had never thought of traveling. Trust the Spirit most of all.

These eight habits of ministry do not provide a way to move a congregation from deep division to wholeness of life. For that, conflict-management consultants have a dozen other strategies. These are rather leadership principles that can help you and the congregation find a way to embrace conflict in a way that deepens community.

However, we who lead congregations need to understand that some issues stand beyond conflict. Some conflict is healthy, a sign that people care. Some conflict is lethal. Author and pastoral counselor G. Lloyd Rediger's book *Clergy Killers*[1] explains that some people in our congregations are dangerous. Some are emotionally ill. Others have a problem with authority figures who remind them of an abusive parent. Not all conflict is an opportunity for pastoral care. Conflict created by these lethal parishioners will do you in. The pastor is the most vulnerable figure in the church. Accuse her of being a gossip, accuse him of having an affair with a parishioner, start a rumor—and it is all over. In every one of those examples, the pastor stands guilty by accusation. Every experienced pastor can name the clergy killers in each congregation he or she has served. Here is what I believe to be the defense:

- Recognize the danger early. Learn to distinguish lethal from healthy conflict. If one person opposes the pastor on every issue, if there is never any logic behind the opposition, if you are the last to hear about the parishioner's problem with you, if this opponent won't let go of the complaint to consider an alternative or accept an apology — if there is a combination of any or all of these factors, watch out.
- With people you think might pose a danger, be clinical, do everything by the book, and share as little of yourself as possible.
- Create a paper trail. Take notes of every contact with dates and a verbatim account, and keep those notes locked in a safe place for a long time.
- Most important, build a strong support system within the church.

Your only real security is the public knowledge that many strong
people are ready and able to defend you. That knowledge will
prompt these people to look for another, more vulnerable authority
figure to victimize.

Lee, my defensiveness may surprise you. You think of me as being
open and vulnerable to people. But I cannot be so to people I believe are
out to hurt or destroy me. The trick is to see the difference and to be
open and vulnerable with the vast majority who are healthy and eager
for a meaningful relationship. Some pastors have been hurt so deeply
that they mistrust everyone. That is a sad condition. It is also a sign that
it is time to move on to another congregation or vocation.

As you decide how to proceed with this "Open and Affirming" proposal, remember that there is no right or wrong way. Whatever you do,
understand the issue of conflict for what it is, and search for the truth. Is
it a dangerous threat to your ministry or a wonderful opportunity for the
Gospel?

Yours in the grace of Jesus Christ,

Paul

CHAPTER 15

Evangelism

November 19

Dear Lee,

I am glad to hear that life is going well at Central Church. The stewardship drive is underway; the Christian education program isn't perfect,
but people seem satisfied with what is being offered; the group of three
who raised the possibility of becoming an "Open and Affirming Congregation" were excited to gain your support and yet seemed sensitive to
the issues that this initiative will evoke. Most of all, I am happy that you
are energized by your work there and that you understand you are really
making a difference in the lives of both families and institutions. What
more could one ask at the end of six months? Now several people new to
the congregation have come, and you are wondering whether the wider
church can offer any wisdom about membership development.

A lively debate is going on in the church about evangelism. Some
people, many of them the scholars I respect most, contend that there is a
difference between evangelism and church growth. Evangelism spreads
the good news of the Gospel and invites people into the Christian faith.
Church growth is the institutional church's effort to welcome new members. Those who make this distinction say that evangelism precedes
church growth, and that if we blend the two, we trivialize both. They
fear that if church growth equals evangelism, then evangelism will take
a back seat to the institutional inclination to increase membership for
the sake of meeting the budget. That is not my point of view. Rather, I
agree with the apostle Paul's strategy of inviting people into the faith by
inviting them into the church. As in Paul's day, many modern churches

are divided, superficial institutions that have lost any memory of the Gospel. But Paul's strategy grew out of his incarnational theology. God is incarnate in Christ and in the Body of Christ. The way to deepen one's spirituality is to participate in a congregation; the way to learn about Christianity is to be in a church; the way to participate in the mission of God is to join church folk engaged in that mission.

Evangelism and church growth are so linked, in my view, that you should also recall my letters on conflict or Christian education or public worship as you read this. One of the debates in the sixties pitted those who said the church will grow only if there is an active program of evangelism against those who said the church will grow only if it is a vibrant and faithful community. The mainline churches, for the most part, opted for the quality community with no effort to welcome new members. That is one reason we have shrunk in membership. Most of us realize we need both a program of church growth and a community of faith.

All the techniques of church growth described in this letter will be a shallow pretense if you don't have an adult-education program that helps people articulate their faith so clearly that they can say to a neighbor, "I believe in Jesus Christ because . . . .Why don't you come with me on Sunday and see what I mean?" The best strategies for growth will amount to nothing if healthy conflict in the church turns lethal. New members always bring change, simply because they also bring a different culture to the church. A growing church needs to know how to deal with conflict. The best program of church growth will be useless if the community hasn't decided what it is, how it plans to move into the future, and why all this is important theologically.

The context of life in this country these days makes my point about the relationship between evangelism and church growth even more crucial. A deep hunger in the United States makes this the pregnant moment for the evangelical task. Individualism has deepened in our society. Many people have no community at all. This loneliness makes the Christian community more attractive than ever. Cynicism is everywhere evident. Few believe in anything or anyone. Institutions that held us together in times past are dying because no one believes in them anymore. A church that believes, hopes, and lives for the good news of Jesus Christ is a welcome community indeed.

Spirituality is "in" because people are starved for meaning in a world that seems increasingly absurd. Every publisher knows that religion sells; why does the church assume it doesn't? If we connect the church and the faith of Jesus Christ, we will be a church that is evangelical, a church that spreads the Gospel. Therefore, it is urgent that you understand that church growth and evangelism are one.

The members of Central Church say they want to attract new members. I'll bet that issue came up in your interview with the search committee. But do they really mean it? If you had a membership increase of 30 percent in the first year of your ministry, would they be happy? I suspect not. They would complain that the new folk get all the attention and that no one notices the long-time members anymore. The fact that no growth has occurred is evidence of this ambivalence. I know the town isn't growing. But the evidence nationwide is that people are looking for spiritual answers. Some of those people must live within driving distance of Central Church.

The first task is to teach the congregation how to grow. It's not that you do this first and then welcome newcomers after the church is educated. The education happens as new people are sought and integrated into the congregation. I put this teaching piece first because it is an imperative. The church will not grow without this education. Here are some ways to make that happen.

1. Emphasize the theological call to hospitality through your preaching, teaching, and church newsletter articles. Look at the way Jesus risked his life in welcoming outsiders. He welcomed all kinds of people—rich and poor, handicapped and able-bodied, those with great reputations and those, like the woman at the well, who were shunned.

2. Ask recent visitors how the congregation greeted them, and share that feedback with members in the newsletter. We gathered recent visitors once or twice a year in the church parlor after worship and asked them for honest feedback. You might develop a letter asking how they were greeted in the sanctuary, at the coffee hour, in the church school, or by the pastor. Criticism by these recent visitors will be shocking to long-time members. But they need to hear that visitors found the coffee hour a cold and intimidating gathering at which church members talked only to people they knew, that no one bothered to get the newcomers' names and addresses, or that they had expected a letter following their visit.

3. Create a profile of church members who intentionally welcome new
    visitors to worship on a Sunday morning. The scale runs from (a) to
    (d). Every congregation needs people who fall into each category of
    this profile. My experience is that many people will do (a) and (b),
    but probably only one member can be described by (d).

    (a) This couple welcomes visitors warmly. They exchange names
         and interests and genuinely show how glad they are that these
         visitors came to worship this morning.
    (b) This person does all of (a) and then, after worship, introduces
         visitors to the pastor and walks them down to the coffee hour.
    (c) This young woman does (a) and (b) and proceeds to introduce
         the visitors to church members with whom they might share
         interests. Her husband stays with the visitors while she goes to
         get key church members; then they switch. This couple dedi-
         cates the first 15 minutes of the coffee hour to these visitors.
    (d) This older woman does all of (a), (b), and (c), watches for the
         visitors the next week, tells the pastor if they are absent for
         two weeks running, and encourages everyone else in the con-
         gregation to be more hospitable to strangers.

Here are some other ways to make the church more welcoming:

*   Get a few people to stop by the home of a visitor right after worship
    to say how glad they are to have seen her at worship, to offer him a
    homemade loaf of bread or a jar of jam, and to leave a simple bro-
    chure with names of staff and telephone numbers. All this can be
    done at the front door without going inside.
*   Publish a pictorial directory, and don't be stingy in giving copies
    out to visitors.
*   Ask everyone—member and visitor alike—to wear a name tag. It's
    not a popular request. Many churches give name tags only to
    visitors. But this practice strikes me as backward. After all, visitors
    don't want to be conspicuous, and they are the ones who have the
    most names to remember! We asked members to wear name tags for
    coffee hour, and the congregation automatically started wearing
    them at worship as well. We made the name tags on a computer,
    using a large font readable at a distance, and stored them, by
    family, in a large portable mailbox.

- Make sure the needs of long-time members are met. Gather them for feedback; send birthday cards to those over 80 or 85; make sure those who don't drive can get a ride to church; have a special Sunday to honor 50-year members. Don't let long-time members feel upstaged by newcomers.

The mainline church has been too passive in its evangelism. We need to invite people to come. Here is how one of the churches I served tried to do just that:

1. We tried to look at the program of the church from the newcomer's perspective. Experts consistently point out that growing churches do these three things well:

    - Worship is interesting, innovative, and meaningful.
    - Christian education is excellent—especially for children and youth. Many people who have never been in a church are looking for a good program of Christian nurture for their children.
    - Mission and outreach to the community are active and innovative. People want a church that is involved in service and that cares about the wider community and world.

2. "Image," an advertising term not popular in the church, is important. One of our members put it this way: "We want this to be at least the second-favorite church for everyone in town. We want people, if asked which church in town they have the most favorable impression of, to respond, 'If I were shopping for a faith community other than that to which I belong, I sure would look into Central Church.'"
3. We sent letters to everyone who had bought property in town during the last quarter. The letter welcomed the new homeowners to the community, invited them to our church, and stated clearly that if they were members of another congregation, we looked forward to working with them as we share in the interfaith community in town. A real-estate agent gave us access to names and addresses within the parish zip code range. Some companies will sell you labels. It's a big job but a productive one.
4. Newspapers provide important ways of making your church visible. One church I served paid for advertisements several times during

the year: the week before church school began in September, during Advent and Lent, and preceding a special Sunday. Free newspaper space for announcements is the best advertisement of all. Most churches squander that space with trivia that no one cares about. Use it well. Never miss a deadline. If Central Church isn't listed with the other churches in the weekly religion pages, it looks as if you don't care. We asked a member who wrote well and had connections to the newspaper to report on special events, individuals who were being honored, and exciting programs held by church groups. We included photographs when possible.

5. The second visit is as important as the first. People need to remember the visitor's name. If that doesn't happen, at least have a name tag ready. I usually tried to write after the first visit and call personally after the second.

All the work described so far comes to nothing if you don't integrate newcomers into the life of the church. Match new people up with groups that might interest them: the choir, a women's group, the church school, a Bible study group, a men's breakfast. Tell church members who live near the newcomer that their neighbor visited, and ask them to keep in touch. In seasons when you have several new visitors, hold a meeting after worship to welcome them. Guard against turning this session into a long ad for your church programs. Instead, let the visitors define the subjects covered in the meeting. Make it user-friendly.

The new-member orientation meetings are the focus of this whole venture, as I wrote you in my letter on Christian education on August 5. Be clear about the purpose of these meetings. Every one of them needs to be excellent. People who go away frustrated or bored will never give you a second chance. Complete the integration process in such a way that when people join the church, they feel at home. They have the essential information they need; they have been given offering envelopes and have pledged; they understand whom to approach with a new idea—they are insiders.

As soon as people join the church, invite them to serve in a leadership capacity. Send the biographies of new members to the nominating committee. If they are not placed on standing committees, invite them to serve as ushers, pour coffee, and become identified with those who "run the place."

That might seem like a more ambitious answer than you expected, Lee. But this is a major priority of every church. It is an imperative of the faith.

Thankful for the hospitality of Christ Jesus, I am your fellow newcomer,

Paul

CHAPTER 16

Spirituality of the Clergy

January 5

Dear Lee,

Happy New Year!

Your description of a senior colleague in town who seems to have become bitter, angry, and cynical in the last years of his ministry was moving. How, indeed, do we guard against the loss of vitality, the loss of faith? Compare your colleague with my friend in ministry who seems competent and secure. You know the slick pastor who always knows the right thing to do and say, who isn't really present but keeps running the old tapes. The smooth veneer is another mask hiding pastor from people and from the fearful, awesome word of God. Both of these experienced pastors probably would be well served by a spiritual discipline. I think you are right in naming "spirituality" as a way we stay alive. You are also right that the word *spirituality* is so vague in our time as to be all but unusable. Yet it describes the most important discipline of ministry.

What is spirituality? For me spirituality begins with us, with our innermost soul, with the spirit that defines us. From that human spirit we search for the Spirit of God, the Holy Spirit. That quest for connection, for meaning, and for God is spirituality. Before the Reformation spirituality was the word used to describe the contemplative life. The Reformers rejected the idea that one could plumb the depths of the spirit best from a monastery. The "priesthood of all believers" meant that everyone in the church was a priest, an expert on the subject of spirituality. So the term "spirituality" was replaced by "piety." In our time, the pious soul has become a negative image, that of a priggish, self-righteous person.

Spirituality, then, is a recycled word to describe the inner quest for the Spirit. But already it has become compromised to mean a private, individualized, and self-absorbed quest. Even with all those problems, I still use the word *spirituality* and understand it to be a central discipline of the ministry.

Many pastors feel guilty about their spiritual discipline. The problem is not that these church leaders have no such discipline. Rather, they have a too-narrow definition of spirituality, too often grounded in a discipline that is not authentic to them. For instance, the discipline of meditation is valid for many people as a path toward prayer and a deeper sense of God. But some people have other disciplines to facilitate their prayer lives. To get at this subject I'll divide it into three areas: the culture, the theology, and the practice of spirituality.

First, consider the culture of spirituality. I have heard it said that culture is to humans what water is to a fish. We don't even notice it until we are "out of the water." That is particularly true for those of us who are members of the majority culture. From the first days of our lives, we have been socialized and taught how to respond to life in a certain way. We assume that everyone else in the world was socialized in the way we were. While we were infants, we were taught how to deal with pain, fear, and loneliness; we learned how to laugh, dance, and sing. All that we learned from our parents is part of who we are, our very identity. The culture into which we were socialized shapes the way we respond to God.

Our family and community shaped the culture into which we were socialized. Without being guilty of stereotyping, I can say, for instance, that New England natives are probably more private than public, more shy than extroverted. The poems of Robert Frost give one a good feel for that New England culture. In the same way, those native to Mediterranean cultures are more likely to show their emotions readily and to value community over individuality. If our faith is touched by our culture, then you can assume that the faith of a New Englander will look different from the faith of a Mediterranean native. Most people assume everyone's faith is, or ought to be, acculturated the same way as their own. The truth is that within the Christian faith there is no one right cultural response to God, no culture that can be defined as Christian. From the very beginning, the Christian faith has been cross-cultural. St. Paul included both Jewish and Greek culture in the church.

There is no right discipline for your spiritual quest, Lee. Some people use the disciplines of yoga and meditation as their spiritual tools. Others study, discuss, think. The only rule is that the discipline needs to be yours. If you try to copy someone else's culture, someone else's spiritual discipline, it won't work. We can learn from one another, but in the end, it must be our own unique quest.

Our cultural experiences will in turn inform our theology of spirituality. My memory of Theology 101 all those years ago identifies three vehicles by which we know the authoritative truth of God: the Bible, our experience, and the church.

The Bible is the obvious way we hear God's Word. Augustine, Martin Luther, and Karl Barth are three examples of people who reached beyond themselves to the power of God by reading the Scriptures. All three demonstrate the power of Pauline theology. Consider the wonderful story of Lloyd VanVactor, a missionary of the United Church Board for World Ministries, who was captured and held hostage for months in the South Pacific. Lloyd befriended the young radicals who held him at gunpoint and offered them admission to the school where he taught when the ordeal was over. During his imprisonment, the one thing available to him to read was a Bible. He decided it would be revealing to read the letters of Paul there in his imprisonment, since so many of Paul's epistles were written from prison. Those letters showed Lloyd how he could rejoice in God's grace, even while in prison, and that is what kept him alive and sane all those months. We may not be in prison, but Paul can help keep us sane too, as we recall our reliance on God's grace. Find time to read the Bible—Old and New Testament, gospels and epistles. Look at the commentaries; bring all the scholarship you developed at seminary to the table. Then read imaginatively. See yourself in the action. Understand it is not just *a* story, it is *our* story.

Experience is the second way we know God—not secondhand experience, but personal, firsthand. My call to ministry shaped my habitual experience of the sacred. I was an awkward 13-year-old with a bad stutter and a severe learning disability. One day our pastor, John Martin, came to see my mother, who chaired the Christian education committee. At the end of their visit, I was asked to come to the door to say goodbye. As he was leaving, John said, over my head to my mother, "Paul would make a wonderful minister." When he was gone, my mother and I had a good laugh. Imagine me, stuttering, hating to read, unable to make a close friend, becoming a minister. But from that moment on, through prep school, college, and army, I found myself comparing every possible career to that of pastor. John had seen in me what no one else saw, and I finally caved in to that call. That is what has made all the difference. My call to ministry came through the church, through the pastor, John Martin.

Given that experience, God's Word is most often made incarnate to me in human community. But solitude is also required if the heart is to be touched. Therefore, I try to take time to be alone, free of tasks and the burdens of the day, time to be. I also try to put myself into a place where God can speak through others—a small group, a continuing-education class, a place where I can listen to loved ones who care enough about me to speak truthfully.

The church is the third vehicle of God's word. Remember that the Bible, the earliest canon, was formed by the church. Most of us know that the Bible comes to life in the context of the church, as in Bible study groups or public worship. Our experience also must be tested by church tradition. Experiencing the risen Christ on the Damascus Road didn't of itself make Paul an apostle. The blinding experience had to be tested and informed by the church in Jerusalem. Our sense that God wanted us to serve in the ordained ministry wasn't enough. That experience had to be tested by the church before ordination could become a reality. That is the problem with the way spirituality is defined these days. Too often, it is such a private, individual experience that people don't feel the need to relate to either the Scripture or the tradition of the faith community. Take time to be a member of the Body of Christ—not just to lead, preach, and teach the church, but to be a parishioner, a disciple, a hearer of the Word. Be clear about who the pastor is for Chris and you. It might be the denominational figure named to be "pastor to pastors," or someone of your own choosing. To be a pastor, one must also be a parishioner.

Bible, experience, church—you have seen how impossible it is to separate any of these from the other two. While we enter the discipline of spirituality from our own culture and personal inclination, the Spirit opens the whole range to us.

Finally, our cultural roots and theology are expressed through our practice of spirituality. The connection between body and spirit is irrefutable. The Christian faith is not dualistic about this truth. The activity of our soul is linked to the activity of our body. Eastern religious meditation makes this point as well: the body at rest and the receptive soul are connected to each other. Whatever your discipline, that same truth must be honored.

But don't limit the physical posture that will open your spirit. One colleague in ministry whom I respect prays to God while swimming. That is the body posture that links her to God's Spirit. If you think about the first months in the water of our mother's womb, where God knit us together, that makes sense. Others meditate on the run—literally. While jogging those five miles each morning, they are praying. Bible study is the way I do it, while sitting at a desk. I read myself into the text. I need the Bible to goad and challenge me, to help me transcend myself. Meditation alone doesn't do it for me. Listening to good music, at the concert hall or in worship, can often make things crystal clear for me. Believe it or not, that sort of clarity can come even through music sung poorly by a small volunteer choir, or while one is listening to a bad sermon. But the word of Scripture is always what jolts me to grasp God's will and way.

This matter of spiritual discipline may well address the state of your colleague who is so bitter, angry, and cynical, and of my colleague, who is so slick, practiced, and fake. They have lost their way, their faith, and the real presence of God. To find the way to recovery, to stay connected, to "log in" each day, is to deepen the practice of spirituality.

That is my New Year's resolution: to stay connected, open, and vulnerable.

May the power of that Spirit be with us in this new year,

Paul

CHAPTER 17

Reforming the Congregation

March 2

Dear Lee,

In your letter that came this morning you ask a question that likely will haunt you all your days: "How can I move this congregation away from the country-club culture to being a faith community?" You observe that the Christian faith is not a subject that people talk about anywhere except in the adult-education class. You are right: There are not many occasions for conversation about the Christian faith, and people rarely take advantage of the occasions that arise. Given that fact of mainline church life, how can you lead the congregation toward being a community of faith?

You have put your finger on a central issue of church life in this country today. Ironically, in a time when religious books are at their most popular, when so many are embarked on urgent spiritual searches, when God is the topic on so many talk shows, people in churches remain shy about speaking of religion.

We must first try to understand, without being judgmental and condemning, why church people are so hesitant to speak of God. After all, this question is about *us*, not just "those" people. We join a church for a lot of different reasons, all of which are good:

- We search for community. As our culture values individuality more and more, we are increasingly lonely, afraid, and anxious. All of us are on an urgent quest for community in which there is acceptance, affirmation, forgiveness, and love. We are all looking for an extended family that cares. A parish church promises to provide that community, that affirmation, that love.

- We want a place where our children will be nurtured in the faith. That is why so many young adults join a church right after the birth of their first child. But it isn't only young adults who want a Christian education for their children. People of all age groups understand the importance of developing a deeper understanding of their faith.
- We want to be a part of a community that shares our values. Especially in a time when there are seems to be no consensus about what is true, important, or worthy, we are looking for support in our quest for a value system and the courage to stand firm for those values.
- We want personal wholeness. All of us know what brokenness means. We suffer from ill health, grief, addiction, abuse, rejection, and disillusionment. We have to get our lives together somehow. Joining a church is a good first step.
- We want to find courage within ourselves to live life with integrity. When the whole culture is running against the things we value, when society is headed in the opposite direction, how can we find the courage to be true to ourselves?

None of that requires an exploration into the meaning of God. Many "successful" churches satisfy those who are searching for all these things without ever dealing seriously with spirituality, prayer, Christian doctrine, or the faithful life. Lee, you and I agree that those churches are fraudulent; we believe that the best way to address all those worthy needs is to address our need for God. But *how* we do that is your question. It is a question about spirituality—the spirituality of the church itself.

I think Walter Wink, in his books *Naming the Powers* (1984) and *Unmasking the Powers* (1986), is most helpful in understanding this question.[1] We have all had the experience he describes. In some congregations the old-timers always talk nostalgically about the good old days. As much as we love and appreciate these people, we often long to be free of this anchor to the past that seems to tie us down. Then, we notice to our horror that the new people who just joined the church, people who had never belonged to any church until two short years ago, have begun to talk fondly about "the way we used to do things." In joining the church they were assimilated into the culture of the place and captured by the spirit (or as Wink calls it, "the angel") of the congregation. As the author of the book of Revelation addressed letters "to the angel of the church in Ephesus," Wink suggests we need to preach not only to the people but also to the angel of the church. These angels (or, to use Paul's image, the principalities and powers) are powerful indeed, but they are subject to the power of Christ. But the angel is not converted overnight. That's why I believe in long pastorates. In the first decade, we are able to help couples, families, and individuals; in the second decade we are able to open the institution itself to change. While most of our training is for the first decade, the work of the second decade, the ministry to the angel, is the most lasting.

Rona Anderson, a former student of mine, wrote a beautiful paper in which she applied Walter Wink's insights to her home church; she calls it "St. A's." She looked at that church using each of the six outer manifestations of the spirit Wink proposes:

- The architecture and ambiance of the place.
- The makeup of the congregation—class, education, race, gender balance.
- The power structures of the congregation—just where is the power?
- How the congregation handles conflict.
- The liturgy, music, preaching, educational programs, and theology.
- How the church sees itself and is seen by others.

Then Rona responded to Wink's question, "If you drew the angel, what colors would you choose?" This is what she saw:

As I thought about drawing the angel, an image formed of a slender, male figure, seen from the side. He has one knee to the ground, his back is curved and stooped, and the wing that is toward me is lifted, hiding his face. He wears a rich, dark red brocade robe, and his wing feathers are a soft grayish white. This image is very expressive to me, of richness and beauty combined with deep interiority and a refusal to see.

Wink has specific advice about how to deal with the angel.

Churches are like people: they do not change in order that they might be accepted; they must be accepted in order that they might change.[2]

The angel, it is important to stress, is not an agent of change. . . .
The angel must receive a message from the Human Being (son of
man) through the prophetic intermediary.[3]

The angel of a church becomes demonic when the congregation
turns its back on the specific tasks set before it by God and makes
some other goal its idol.[4]

To all of that, Rona responds:

I think St. A's is badly out of balance. . . . Returning to my visual
image of the angel, it seems more and more clear to me that the best
thing for me to do is to try to get the angel to lower its wing, even if
only a little, and begin to see.

Wink describes the paradox this way:

We must do everything we can to foster change, and we can do
nothing. God calls us to transform the church, and yet only God can
bring that transformation about. God sends us to proclaim the word,
and we are utterly free of any responsibility to make the word effective. When we can live within that paradox without incredulity,
we will discover that God is indeed the real sovereign of the world.[5]

The most important conflict is the struggle between the Holy Spirit
and the principalities and powers that have a grip on both the church and
on those of us who are leaders in the church. That is the spiritual issue.

It is hard to address these big issues partly because they have no
readily available, easy answers. People prefer to talk only of those things
about which they have some knowledge. So the conversation in the coffee hour or in the church parking lot is most often about politics, public-
school policy, the health-care system, work, or family life. People feel
uncomfortable when the talk turns to religion because they are afraid of
showing their ignorance. In this past decade more and more young adults
joined the church with no religious background at all. Many of their
parents had left the church in the sixties, so their children had literally
never been inside a church before becoming adults. One young professional who was not raised in the church explained to me how he memorized the Lord's Prayer on the commuter train. These people turned the

culture of the congregation around. In generations past, when people talked about their faith, they shared convictions: "I believe that . . ." These new members had no such convictions about the faith. Instead they had questions—wonderful, insightful, difficult questions that started with "Why." Why is there such injustice? Why is life so unfair? Why does God allow this behavior? Why is the church the way it is? Gradually, people started to value the ability to ask the questions even when there were no easy answers. That cultural shift is perhaps the most important way we approach the faith issues—by honoring the question as much as the answer.

The church can refocus its attention through a "visioning process." Every time I have been part of such a venture, it has changed the church. There is nothing magic about it. Rather, it is an attempt to get the whole church to think about the mission of the church for a sustained period of time with the specific task of creating, in the end, a mission or vision statement or a church covenant.

We used to think about strategic planning for the future—five or ten years into the future. "What do we want to be like then?" was the question. Some of us felt it was the leader's responsibility to envision that future and to persuade the whole institution to follow him or her toward it. Margaret Wheatley's wonderful contribution to this dialogue, *Leadership and the New Science,*[6] helped me see this process in a new light. Wheatley believes that a new field of vision in the here and now marks the new beginning toward the future.

In my view, the Protestant Reformation can illustrate Dr. Wheatley's point. The Reformers didn't have a clear view into the future. They had a field of vision in their present. They understood themselves, the church, and the Gospel in a fresh and new way; that's what led to the Reformation. That is what leads a congregation toward reformation also.

Begin by naming a small steering committee made up of a cross section of church leaders. I believe it is worth engaging someone from outside the church as a consultant, someone who knows what resources are available and who has not been influenced by the angel of this particular congregation. The scope of the study will include a study of the community, providing the context of the congregation; a summary of the congregation's history; worship and Bible study that connect the congregation to the call of God; gatherings in homes, where people can share not only their values and dreams, but also their understandings of who God calls us to be as a church. The pastor is not the one to do this work and sell it to the congregation. Rather, the pastor is called to gather people from across the church. When people gather in all their diversity to ask who they are, clarity comes, by the grace of God. Out of that self-understanding, out of that new field of vision, comes a path to the future.

Yours is the key ongoing question for ministry: "How can I move this congregation away from the country-club culture to being a faith community?" How are we different from the Rotary Club, the golf and tennis clubs, and the newcomers club? Who are we as a church? What is God calling us to be and do? When we ask those questions and let them ferment within and among us, the Holy Spirit works her way toward reformation. That is a great agenda for the 2nd through the 42nd year of your ministry.

With admiration and enthusiasm,

Paul

CHAPTER 18

Continuing Growth for the Pastor

April 28

Dear Lee,

I imagine the fact that I have not heard from you for all these weeks is a sign that things are going well for you. The frantic days of Lent are past, and I'm sure you have been simply too busy to write. Your letter describing the pastor in town who had become so bitter and angry, on the other hand, has haunted me. Why is it that some people become cynical and hostile at the end of their ministry while others are energized and excited all the way to the final farewell reception? That is the question I have been focused on this winter. I have read, listened to colleagues, talked with seminary professors and denominational executives. I have some ideas on the subject. I share them with you because this is your issue: What do you need to do now to prevent serious burnout 20 or 30 years from now?

Almost everything has changed in this country and the church since I was ordained in 1959. We have totally different attitudes than we once had toward love, sex, power, institutions, money, religion, and our very identity. Moreover, in the church the meaning of ministry has shifted. Parishioners act more self-absorbed, feel more entitled, and seem far more inclined to protect their rights and privileges by suing any and all adversaries, including you, Lee. Why is it that some pastors thrive in this atmosphere while others are crushed by it?

At first, I thought it was a matter of expectations: that the burnt-out ones were those who had expected to proceed on the fast track from small-town pastor to bishop, those who had expected to be honored as leader, those with a romantic view of ministry who became jaded and hurt when things didn't work out as they had planned. But that just isn't true. All of the people I have talked with who thrive in their last years of ministry claim they had all the wrong expectations at the start. Remember my expectation that I would be like the pastor of my childhood church—the most popular man in town? Everyone is guilty, in the beginning, of a heroic and romantic image of "the great pastor."

Why do some thrive in this environment that seems so hostile to others? Here is the answer I would advance: Successful pastors are lifelong learners. When the old tricks no longer work, they love a new challenge, a new situation to understand theologically, a new set of skills to learn. The young adult who feels so entitled is a gift to the lifelong learner. Why does she think this way? How can I help her see the difference between feeling entitled to "my rights" and feeling thankful to God for so many gifts? The survivors in ministry are perennial students who embrace the new upside-down career track, where the best among us don't even seek the position of senior minister or bishop. They talk about how much they can learn from young graduates, two-career families, or new immigrants.

To put it simply: When everything has changed so completely that the old ways of being a pastor no longer work, some people get cynical and angry because they are left out, while others are energized by the opportunity to learn a new way of being a pastor.

What does all that mean to you, Lee, in your first year of your first church? It means you need to understand the ministry as discipleship. We must become learners, or we are sunk. Therefore, our lifelong learning patterns become all-important. Those who survive are those who are always growing, always learning.

Educator Thomas Armstrong has written a book, *Multiple Intelligences in the Classroom*,[1] based on the theory of multiple intelligences advanced by Howard Gardner, professor of education at the Harvard Graduate School of Education. I think we need to take this idea into the discipline of ministry. "Multiple Intelligences in the Ministry" might have been the title of this letter! I will quote Armstrong's summary of Gardner's seven intelligences and add my application to ministry below.

- **Linguistic Intelligence:** "The capacity to use words effectively, whether orally (e.g., as a storyteller, orator, or politician) or in

writing (e.g., as a poet, playwright, editor, or journalist) ."
This, of course, is the pastor's trade. Sermon preparation, reflections in the newsletter, and the ability to tell a story well are daily tasks in the parish ministry.

- **Logical-Mathematical Intelligence:** "The capacity to use numbers effectively (e.g., as a mathematician, tax accountant, or statistician) and to reason well (e.g., as a scientist, computer programmer, or logician)."
  The two skills the pastor needs to excel in ministry fall within this intelligence. (1) The ability to create and understand the church budget: If we haven't a clue what that budget is about, we are vulnerable. (2) The ability to communicate with those in the congregation who operate from this intelligence most comfortably: If we are able to function only from our right-brain preference, half the congregation will forever be strangers to us.

- **Spatial Intelligence:** "The ability to perceive the visual-spatial world accurately (e.g., as a hunter, scout, or guide) and to perform transformations upon those perceptions (e.g., as an interior decorator, architect, artist, or inventor)."
  I am convinced that the mystery of God, the meaning of the sacred, the power of the spirit is grasped, in part at least, with this spatial intelligence. We need to make visible the symbols; we need to guide the pilgrimage; we need to use the language and symbol of space and time to make the faith real.

- **Bodily-Kinesthetic Intelligence:** "Expertise in using one's whole body to express ideas and feelings (e.g., as an actor, a mime, an athlete, or a dancer) and facility in using one's hands to produce or transform things (e.g., as a craftsperson, sculptor, mechanic, or surgeon)."
  This intelligence is more significant than gesture. We pastors need to understand the power of liturgical dance, the power of architecture, a sense of how things go together. If the Christ is to be incarnate in our midst, this intelligence is near the center of our work.

- **Musical Intelligence:** "The capacity to perceive (e.g., as a music aficionado), discriminate (e.g., as a music critic), transform (e.g., as a composer), and express (e.g., as a performer) musical forms." *This intelligence is more than getting along with the organist. Music is probably a more significant way of communicating the Gospel than words. We need to be a part of the music-leadership team, we need to pay attention to the selection of hymns, and we need to understand how church music and the Christian life are connected.*

- **Interpersonal Intelligence:** "The ability to perceive and make distinctions in moods, intentions, motivations and feelings of other people." *This is the intelligence of our trade. Everything from pastoral care to stewardship, education, mission, and leadership itself depends on this intelligence. Without keen interpersonal skills we are not able to function as church leaders.*

- **Intrapersonal Intelligence:** "Self-knowledge and the ability to act adaptively on the basis of that knowledge."[2] *In my view, the first six intelligences depend on this seventh. The foundation of ministry is this self-knowledge.*

What is new about Howard Gardner's list is his insistence that all seven are *intelligences*. You've heard people say, "He's not very intelligent, but he has a wonderful aptitude for music" (or a great talent as an artist or athlete). Gardner declares:

1. Each person possesses all seven intelligences.
2. Most people can develop each intelligence to an adequate level of competency.
3. Intelligences usually work together in complex ways.
4. There are many ways to be intelligent within each category. For example, an illiterate person can be a great storyteller.[3]

You can see how each intelligence is related to the work of the pastor. Excellence in ministry demands growth in all seven intelligences. Furthermore, all seven develop together. Remember how surprised you were in high school to discover that when you took time away from studies to play on the basketball team, you were able to learn more in less study time? When I say we need to continue learning, I mean we should continue developing all seven intelligences. When we join a community-theater group, we are not shortchanging our ministry. The linguistic excellence of our sermons will be enhanced by the time we spend at the art class or at the gym.

When we grow, in this total sense of the word, we grow as persons. That is what keeps us true to our calling, after all is said and done—not improving our techniques as professionals but developing our authenticity as whole persons.

When I was 50, I thought about leaving the ministry to do something else for the rest of my working life. I went to a career-counseling center, where I took all the tests imaginable. On the last day, a psychologist spent the afternoon sharing with me the results of these instruments. It was a wonderful experience that convinced me I was in the right career. The psychologist told me, "Paul, you thrive when you are living and working with people who are smarter than you. You are happiest when you have to scramble to keep up. When you retire, be sure you don't end up as the big fish in the little pool."

That challenge was addressed to me. It rings true. I live by it. The question is, "What is your unique growth pattern?" I believe Howard Gardner is right in his theory that each person possesses all seven intelligences. He acknowledges that each of us is stronger in one or two of the seven than in the rest. Which intelligences will you scramble to keep up with? Our first inclination is to go with our strength, but we also need to work on the intelligences that are least developed. We need to keep on learning and growing if we are to keep on living. We become angry old cynics within a year of the day we stop learning. Why is it that some pastors thrive in these challenging times while others are crushed? The simple answer is that those who thrive are those who strive to keep on growing.

Your fellow student,

Paul

Thanks To You, Lee, and Others

May 17

Dear Lee,

I am absolutely overwhelmed. I can't believe you saved all these letters and sent them off to a publisher. The Alban Institute is prepared to publish them in the spring. If I had known you were going to do this, I might have written these notes more carefully!

In fact, since I have heard of your clever scheme, I have sent the letters to Carole Carlson, Ben Griffin, Chuck Harper, and Brita Gill-Austern, who have graciously read them and made suggestions. Two editors at the Alban Institute have worked with me: Beth Ann Gaede, who helped me shape the original book proposal, and David Lott, who has been polishing the final manuscript. I am grateful to them all.

These letters were possible because of a host of people. Jackie lived this life with me and has read each letter as she read each sermon along the way. I would not be writing to you if it were not for her support and love. Elizabeth Nordbeck, dean of the faculty and vice president for academic affairs at Andover Newton Theological School, asked me to teach a course on the "Practicalities of Parish Ministry" five years ago. Her faith in me, as well as in my co-teacher, Elizabeth King, pastor of the Tabernacle Church in Salem, Massachusetts—not to mention all the students in those classes—made these letters possible. Finally, I also thank the clergy colleagues and people in the three churches I have served in Massachusetts. I learned more from them than from all the courses I have ever taken and all the books I've read. Nevertheless,

I am enclosing with this letter a short bibliography of those books that have influenced me.

So now, these letters, written to you, Lee, are to become public. I will close with a word to all who will look over our shoulders and read our correspondence.

God bless you all in the ministry of Jesus Christ. May you be as happy in your life as a pastor as I have been, and in the end may you be as sure of God's grace as I am this day.

Lee, thank you a thousand times.

With love,

Paul

NOTES

Introduction

1. Dietrich Bonhoeffer, *Life Together* (New York: Harper & Brothers, 1954), 29-30.

Chapter 3

1. William H. Willimon, *Clergy and Laity Burn-Out* (Nashville: Abingdon Press, 1989).

Chapter 4

1. R. Paul Stevens and Phil Collins, *The Equipping Pastor: A Systems Approach to Congregational Leadership* (Bethesda, Md.: Alban Institute, 1993).

2. Stevens and Collins, *Equipping Pastor,* 41.

3. Stevens and Collins, *Equipping Pastor,* xiii.

4. Stevens and Collins, *Equipping Pastor,* 45.

5. Stevens and Collins, *Equipping Pastor,* 3.

6. Stevens and Collins, *Equipping Pastor,* 55.

Chapter 5

1. Quoted in Stevens and Collins, *Equipping Pastor*, 119.

Chapter 6

1. Many good resources are available. One I particularly recommend is David Glusker and Peter Misner, *Words for Your Wedding: The Wedding Service Book* (San Francisco: HarperSanFrancisco, 1994).

Chapter 8

1. Ruth Duck, *Gender and the Name of God: The Trinitarian Baptismal Formula* (Cleveland: Pilgrim Press, 1991).

2. Duck, *Gender and the Name of God*, 159.

3. Duck, *Gender and the Name of God*, 163.

Chapter 10

1. From comments by Colleen Stiriti, director of educational ministries, Congregational Church of Needham (United Church of Christ), Needham, Mass.

Chapter 11

1. For more information on *Called to Care*, call (800) 325-7061. Stephen Ministry can be reached at (314) 428-2600.

Chapter 13

1. Paul C. Clayton, *Mission: A Parish Perspective* (Cleveland: Stewardship Council of the United Church of Christ, 1993). Now out of print, it is available from the bookstore at Andover Newton Theological School, 210 Herrick Road, Newton Centre, MA 02459.

Chapter 14

1. G. Lloyd Rediger, *Clergy Killers: Guidance for Pastors and Congregations Under Attack* (Louisville: Westminster John Knox Press, 1997).

Chapter 17

1. Walter Wink, *Naming the Powers: The Language of Power in the New Testament* (Philadelphia: Fortress Press, 1984) and *Unmasking the Powers: The Invisible Forces That Determine Human Existence* (Philadelphia: Fortress Press, 1986).

2. Wink, *Unmasking the Powers*, 81.

3. Wink, *Unmasking the Powers*, 80.

4. Wink, *Unmasking the Powers*, 78.

5. Wink, *Unmasking the Powers*, 82.

6. Margaret Wheatley, *Leadership and the New Science: Learning about Organization from an Orderly Universe* (San Francisco: Berrett-Koehler Publishers, 1994).

Chapter 18

1. Thomas Armstrong, *Multiple Intelligences in the Classroom* (Alexandria, Va.: Association for Supervision and Curriculum Development, 1994).

2. The quotations on pp. 110-112 are from Armstrong, *Multiple Intelligences in the Classroom*, 2-3.

3. Armstrong, *Multiple Intelligences in the Classroom*, 11-12.

BIBLIOGRAPHY

Armstrong, Thomas. *Multiple Intelligences in the Classroom*. Alexandria, Va.: Association for Supervision and Curriculum Development, 1994.

Bonhoeffer, Dietrich. *Life Together*. New York: Harper & Brothers, 1954.

Bosch, David. *Transforming Mission: Paradigm Shifts in Theology of Mission*. Maryknoll, N.Y.: Orbis Books, 1991.

Callahan, Kennon L. *Effective Church Leadership: Building on the Twelve Keys*. San Francisco: HarperSanFrancisco, 1990.

Clayton, Paul C. *Mission—A Parish Perspective*. Cleveland: Stewardship Council of the United Church of Christ, 1993.

Covey, Steven R. *The 7 Habits of Highly Effective People: Powerful Lessons in Personal Change*. New York: Simon & Schuster, 1989.

Duck, Ruth. *Gender and the Name of God: The Trinitarian Baptismal Formula*. Cleveland: Pilgrim Press, 1991.

Foltz, Nancy T., ed. *Religious Education in the Small Membership Church*. Birmingham, Ala.: Religious Education Press, 1990.

Friedman, Edwin H. *Friedman's Fables*. New York/London: Guilford Press, 1990.

Friedman, Edwin H. *Generation to Generation: Family Process in Church and Synagogue*. New York: Guilford Press, 1985.

Glusker, David, and Peter Misner. *Words for Your Wedding: The Wedding Service Book*. San Francisco: HarperSanFrancisco, 1994.

Hahn, Celia Allison. "Losing Control—And Gaining Authority." *The Christian Ministry* (January-February 1995), 11-14.

Roehlkepartain, Eugene C., and Donald L. Gregg. *The Teaching Church: Moving Christian Education to Center Stage.* Nashville: Abingdon Press, 1993.

Stevens, R. Paul, and Phil Collins. *The Equipping Pastor: A Systems Approach to Congregational Leadership.* Bethesda, Md.: Alban Institute, 1993.

Wheatley, Margaret. *Leadership and the New Science: Learning about Organization from an Orderly Universe.* San Francisco: Berrett-Koehler Publishers, 1994.

Willimon, William H. *Clergy and Laity Burn-Out.* Creative Leadership Series. Nashville: Abingdon Press, 1989.

Willimon, William H. *Remember Who You Are: Baptism and the Christian Life.* Nashville: Upper Room, 1980.

Willimon, William H. *Sunday Dinner.* Nashville: Upper Room, 1981.

Willimon, William H. *Word, Water, Wine, and Bread: How Worship Has Changed Over the Years.* Valley Forge, Pa.: Judson Press, 1980.

Wink, Walter. *Naming the Powers: The Language of Power in the New Testament.* Philadelphia: Fortress Press, 1984.

Wink, Walter. *Unmasking the Powers: The Invisible Forces That Determine Human Existence.* Philadelphia: Fortress Press, 1986.